Discourses of Extremity

Radical Ethics and Post-Marxist Extravagances

NORMAN GERAS

VERSO

London · New York

First published by Verso 1990
© Norman Geras 1990
All rights reserved

Verso
UK: 6 Meard Street, London W1V 3HR
USA: 29 West 35th Street, New York, NY 10001-2291

Verso is the imprint of New Left Books

British Library Cataloguing in Publication Data
Geras, Norman, *1943–*
    Discourses of extremity: radical ethics and post-
    Marxist extravagances.
    1. Marxism. Theories
    I. Title
    335.401

    ISBN 0–86091–266–3
    ISBN 0–86091–980–3 Pbk

US Library of Congress Cataloging-in-Publication Data
Geras, Norman, 1943–
    Discourses of extremity: radical ethics and post-Marxist
    extravagances/Norman Geras.
       p.   cm.
    ISBN 0–86091–266–3. — ISBN 0–86091–980–3 (pbk.)
    1. Socialist ethics.   2. Philosophy, Marxist.   I. Title.
BJ1388.G47   1990
335.4—dc20

Typeset in Baskerville by BP Integraphics Ltd., Bath, Avon
Printed in Great Britain by Bookcraft (Bath) Ltd.

To Sophie and Jenny

Contents

Acknowledgements

'Marxism and Moral Advocacy' was first presented as a paper
to the Symposium on 'Socialist Theory at the End of the Twentieth
Century', held at the University of Groningen in March 1987,
and appears in D. McLellan and S. Sayers, eds, *Socialism and Morality*, Macmillan, London 1990. 'Our Morals' appears in R. Miliband and L. Panitch, eds, *The Socialist Register 1989*, The Merlin
Press, London. 'Post-Marxism?' and 'Ex-Marxism Without Substance' appeared in *New Left Review* nos. 163 and 169, the issues
for May/June of 1987 and 1988 respectively. I am grateful to
the several editors and publishers for permission to use them for
this book.

Introduction

This book attempts to respond to two rather different sorts of exigency confronting socialists today: to be prepared, on the one hand, to make a critical reappraisal of areas of weakness or neglect within the theoretical ideas of socialism, in order to begin to remedy them; and to take care to discriminate, on the other hand, between this needed rethinking of inadequate positions and less salutary pressures upon a valuable theoretical inheritance, pressures of intellectual fashion and reaction. These two tasks are pursued successively in the two halves of the volume. Part One considers problems of Marxist thought in the area of moral or ethical argument, in relation to other – broadly liberal – intellectual perspectives. Part Two treats of a version of so-called 'post-Marxism' and of *its* version of the tradition it wants to leave behind. The book as a whole is concerned with the current status of Marxism, in the light of alternatives to it.

The essays in Part One continue a line of reflection begun in an earlier essay of mine, 'The Controversy About Marx and Justice'. An amplification of the conclusion to that piece, 'Marxism and Moral Advocacy' both registers some of the ways in which Marxism's record on ethical questions has been deficient, and argues for a contrasting strength on its part by comparison with

more overtly ethical discourses. The issues are focused via a consideration of the problem of world hunger. It is other such moral
extremities, conditions of tyranny or grave injustice, that are at
the heart also of the following essay, 'Our Morals'. This examines
traditional socialist arguments about the permissible means of
revolutionary change, in order to demonstrate their radical insuf-
ficiency. It suggests there is something important to be learned
in the matter from another tradition of thought about violent
human conflict.

Part Two brings together my contributions to a recent debate
in the pages of *New Left Review*. 'Post-Marxism?', which initiated
it, is an extensive critique of Ernesto Laclau and Chantal Mouffe's
book, *Hegemony and Socialist Strategy*. The essay evoked a somewhat
abusive and thoroughly evasive 'reply' on their part, to which
'Ex-Marxism Without Substance' rejoins. The two essays together
rebut Laclau and Mouffe's account of the Marxist tradition and
the 'discourse' theory they would have displace it, highlighting
in the process the extreme arbitrariness and excess within their
own discourse. Laclau and Mouffe's theoretical positions today,
of little weight in themselves, are nevertheless exemplary in a
number of ways. These writers express in the purest form an
old critical strategy against Marxism: to represent it as essentially
crude, oversimplified, reductionist and so forth, by just writing
out of Marxism everything within the tradition that is otherwise;
so what is there is either impoverished or it is not really Marxism.
And they also exemplify, in the one place, *two* well-known routes
taken by intellectuals breaking with Marxism when − as is not
always the case − they are unable to give a straightforward account
to themselves and others of what they are doing. The one route
is, as if by a sudden, transforming insight, to begin to disparage
the whole body of ideas, so recently one's own, as altogether mis-
taken or worthless or dangerous. The other route is to 'develop',
as it were sympathetically, the tradition from within − so as to
leave virtually nothing of it intact. These routes are generally
taken by different people, but it is a convenient ambiguity of the
'post-Marxist' rubric that it makes it possible for one to tread

both of them simultaneously, being now 'post-', and now '-Marxist', as required.

One hope in putting this volume together has been that, beyond the specific concerns and arguments of the separate essays, there might emerge a useful contrast between two different styles of critical approach to the inherited corpus of socialist ideas: one of them committed to analytic care and precision, some real effort of discrimination of respective strengths and weaknesses within competing – complex – bodies of thought; the other ungoverned by any rule of rigour and reckless with the intellectual resources we have. A simple test of this contrast is to consider what resources for its part the outlook criticized in the second half of this book gives for answering the question about socialist ends and means posed in the first half of it.

My principal debt in time and activity of writing is, as ever, to my wife Adèle, whom I thank once again; and then to my daughters, to whom I dedicate this book, with love.

Manchester, April 1989

PART ONE

The Ethics of
Revolution

1

Marxism and Moral Advocacy

Socialist thought in the late twentieth century is assailed by inner
uncertainty as never before. In view of earlier attitudes unnecessary
to rehearse here, this situation obviously has a healthy side to
it. From a certain angle it may even be regarded as a wholly
normal and desirable state of affairs. The available theories of
socialism have never been, nor are they suddenly going to become,
problem-free, and so a measure of reflective scepticism – self-doubt
– is always in order. But not infrequently today one encounters
a sort of guilty breast-beating or hand-wringing within and about
socialist thought, bordering in some cases on virtual self-
abnegation before other intellectual idioms and political outlooks.
This is both unseemly and unnecessary.

In what follows I focus on just one tradition within socialist
thought, namely, Marxism, in an area in which it has been, arguably, at its weakest: namely, ethics.

Let me begin by stating a central thesis of Steven Lukes's lucid
and interesting recent book, *Marxism and Morality*. In a nutshell,
it is that there has been a deep-seated paradox in Marxism's view
of morality, and that this is (only) resolved by attending to a distinction between two *types* of morality. The paradox is this. On the
one hand, Marxism has treated morality as ideological, historically

relative, shaped by social and class determinants, and so on; purporting itself to reject any moral or moralizing discourse, denying that it is based on ideals, and claiming to be scientific. On the other hand, 'Marx's and Marxist writings abound in moral judgements, implicit and explicit'; they present a moral critique of capitalism, together with 'the vision of a better world' which it is 'hard not to see as moral'. All of this is documented by Lukes at length.[1] His proposed resolution of the paradox is that 'it is the morality of *Recht* that [Marxism] condemns as ideological and anachronistic, and the morality of emancipation that it adopts as its own'.[2] In other words: what Marx and later Marxists have treated as historically relative, criticized and often derided, in any case disowned, are moral discourses and systems concerned with rights and obligations and with justice and injustice. Those ethical pronouncements which Marxists have made in their own voice, by contrast, have had to do with values like freedom, self-development or self-realization, and community. This broad distinction is one made by several contributors to recent debates about Marx's attitude to questions of justice.

The case for the existence of the paradox is, in my view, unanswerable. But there are grounds for disputing the resolution Lukes proposes and in fact I do not accept it. Notice, as what may seem a purely formal point, that he does not resolve the paradox *as stated*. For this was that Marxism disparages, not this or that morality or kind of morality, but morality *tout court* – while having recourse simultaneously to moral argument and moral judgement. And, in relation to Karl Marx himself and too many of his followers, that is the plain truth. They have tended to relativize and have belittled – here is the substantive point against Lukes's resolution – not only any ethic of rights or justice, but moral ideals in general, not excluding even that of freedom; and conversely they have condemned capitalism not only for oppressing people, for making or keeping them unfree, but also as being unjust. I have tried to establish this at some length elsewhere, in a survey of the whole debate about Marx and justice, and will not review the arguments and evidence for it here again.[3]

I will only say: the upshot is that the paradox within much Marxist thought is not merely an apparent one, capable of being so 'resolved'. It is a genuine contradiction of belief.

This, then, has been a major weakness within the Marxist tradition, that it at once embodied an ethical dimension and denied it, so obfuscating its own nature and leaving, in the process, some important problems inadequately discussed or not discussed at all. Marxists need to acknowledge that central weakness and begin to make it good. The scientific aspirations and achievements of Marxism are perfectly compatible with its commitment to ethical positions and principles, and these must be stated openly, tested against normative analysis and argument, measured against criticism in the light of other viewpoints, and so forth. The many problematic issues in this area should now receive the attention they deserve. I do not propose to begin that task here, but I will just allude very briefly to two such issues, before going on to sketch in *another* side of the intellectual picture, so to put it. The two issues both concern Marxism's 'vision of a better world'.

The first of them is the question of needs. The satisfaction of human needs has always been a central Marxist principle but this is a notoriously difficult area conceptually. What 'level' of needs is to be satisfied? Marx's own answer to this question was clearly not in any minimalist spirit, as evidenced both by his assumptions about increasing economic productivity and by his constant emphasis on the goal of universal individual self-development. Some would argue, however, that it is only at the level of bare survival needs, if at all, that one can specify an objective schedule of human needs, owing to the very wide diversity of human purposes. Indeed, this line of thought would seem to be supported by notions of historical specificity and cultural relativity that have tended to dominate Marxist thought itself. It is no use appealing, in this context, to a prospective 'abundance' as the future basis for meeting any and every level and content of individual needs. The concept of such unqualified abundance is not merely feeble in the light of contemporary ecological problems and concerns; it has no sense. One can always envisage a set of goals too extravagant in the face of given resources, however richly endowed with these a community may be. The only concept consistent with Marx's, and materialist, assumptions is of a possible sufficiency relative to some standard of 'reasonable' needs.[4] This points, unavoidably, to a necessary process of *social definition* of the level of need satisfaction, a matter to which I shall return in a moment.

The second issue is that of equality. Though some philosophers have argued to the contrary (on the basis of *some* of the things Marx says in this connection), the principle, 'To each according to their needs', is, I contend, an egalitarian one and equality a crucial Marxian value.[5] But it is a problematic value: because equality is always such on some specified dimension(s) and compatible with, or even requiring, inequalities on other dimensions. The slogan, 'To each according to their needs', aims at an equality of welfare rather than, say, exact equality of resources. To that extent, it is conceived as accommodating individuality and variation, and not as a vision of blank uniformity. Would equality of resources be the better or more manageable criterion? Some people may consider it so. If one thinks not, how far can we press inequalities of resources to secure equality of welfare before we begin to doubt that this really is equality of welfare? (For example, imagine someone claiming a more and ever more extravagant arena in which to fulfil her or his creative needs.) Again, how shall we balance up the disbenefits of tedious or unpleasant, but necessary, work tasks against compensating benefits for those who agree to perform them? Such questions raise real theoretical and practical problems for a projected socialism and so need to be further considered and debated. They point, once more, to a necessary process within any emergent socialism of a *social definition* of desirable equalities, allowable inequalities and their limits.

Now, as it does not seem sensible to suppose that any such process of social definition could be purely spontaneous, it must be made explicit that these issues (reasonable needs, desirable equalities, and so on) would have to be matters for a socialist democratic process, matters of public deliberation and decision.

They would be the subjects, that is to say, of a process which is *political*, in one important sense of that word, and not merely administrative. I do not regard this as particularly controversial. It is actually banal; and, furthermore, I take it as only consistent with certain central Marxian beliefs. The state, according to Marx, *in the sense of an organ of class rule and a coercive instrument*, is to give way to a 'public power' which has lost its 'political character';[6] but in *this* particular – Marxist – sense of 'political'. If that is so, if a public power remains, and if the social order of socialism is envisaged as being one both understood (more or less) and consciously shaped by its members, then one cannot foresee a socialism without public affairs, processes of authoritative decision-making – hence politics in an older, classical, sense. One cannot, unless, that is, we just presuppose automatic consensus about everything, which does not seem worth taking seriously. It is only necessary to say any of this at all in order to guard against a way of construing the 'withering away of the state' as implying a time beyond politics, a time of the mere 'administration of things'.

In any case, there is obviously no shortage of problems to be discussed in these areas, much in need of clarification and analysis. We have seen enough of mere slogans and unquestioned dogma. Once this has been said, however, it should also be added: we are entitled to have problems, both theoretical and practical; and open questions and difficulties. No one else is free of them. We can embrace – and have no reason to bewail – our own.

Meanwhile, there *is* another side to this intellectual picture. It may be approached as follows. There were social realities in Marx's day, and there are such in our time as well, enabling one to register a situation of wretched, desperate human need, coexisting with massive inequalities; to register this in advance of the foregoing questions (about standards of need and equality) having been comprehensively analysed. To this extent, although I do not go back on anything argued above, it will not do to pretend that nothing useful can be said prior to resolving all of that. Some Marxists, even, speak sometimes as if the new socialist or communist person, free women and men, would be so transformed and radically different from ourselves that there is not much we can say for and about them; a thought nourished not just by the unexceptionable belief in the historical changeability of human beings but often also by the false argument that Marx had, and Marxism should have, no truck with the idea of a universal human nature.[7] I do not want to quarrel with the proposition that in some, or even many, ways a future socialist populace would be very different from people now. But, in the matter of needs and considering how things presently are, we surely know enough about human beings to be able to say what common, basic human needs must be catered for to make possible a decent human existence for all: adequate nourishment and protection against the elements, therefore housing, clothing, fuel; proper medical care and educational provision; some meaningful and agreeable work; and the possibility – which anyone can refuse – of significant (to large) amounts of time free from work for social, cultural and recreational activities, with some resources given to these ends. (All together, it should be said, with the usual civil and political liberties.)

Suppose everybody had 'only' this. Now, wouldn't that be something! Similarly, when set against the gross and offensive inequalities of present capitalist societies, wouldn't even a rough form of equality, with whatever philosophical complications, be something? Would this all lead, itself, to other – presently unimaginable – utopian heights? Perhaps. But given where we are, we could do with reaching these foothills, a sufficiently inspiring vision in themselves.

The question is *how* to reach them; and here something can be said in partial mitigation of Marxism's habitual reluctance to engage in overt ethical discussion and analysis. For it has been motivated partly by a disdain for *empty* moralizing, by a sense of what I call moral realism. The components of this include: the belief that ideals are by themselves insufficient, mere moral exhortation incapable of accomplishing human liberation; accordingly, a desire and the effort to understand the material conditions of that liberation, including the conditions for transforming moral consciousness; the search, in general, for agencies and movements, ways and means, of bringing revolutionary change about. Strictly, none of this constitutes a good reason for disowning all moral argument, denying one's own ethical standpoint and foregoing careful normative analysis. But to gain some sense of the sort of thing Marx reacted against – in which much of the tradition has followed him – one has only to consider some other, overtly ethical discourses, where justice, obligation, humanity and so on, are explicitly the subject of analysis.

I shall consider two contemporary examples of this here, one to which I confess a strong antipathy, the other essentially decent and much more sympathetic.

According to Robert Nozick's entitlement theory, justice obtains if everyone has come to have what they have in property holdings through roughly-Lockean processes of original acquisition (that is, through appropriating previously unowned natural objects by working on them) and the effects, beyond that, of purely voluntary transfers (exchange, gift, bequest, etc.). He calls the theory a 'historical' one, because in order to know whether someone is entitled to the holdings they have, we need to know the historical path by which these came into their possession. If the paths are 'clean' morally, all titles valid, then things are in order so far as justice goes. The overall *pattern* of property holdings is of no consequence in this. So, if I – or you – through some combination, say, of bad luck, bad judgement and lack of imagination or talent, must live a life of unremitting hardship and wretchedness, while you – or I – thanks to good fortune, sound judgement and keen ability, may enjoy every sort of advantage, comfort and luxury, that is fair; there is no injustice in it. That few socialists are likely to be persuaded by this notion of a just world is not the point here. The point is that, even measured against it, the actual world is pervasively unjust. It is so in at least these ways. (i) There is taxation by states for purposes – such as the provision of welfare services – other than the defence of property rights and, as imposing compulsory transfers, this constitutes an invasion of individual property rights. (ii) Past violations of these rights, and the consequences of them, past and continuing, must be reckoned to have left a mark: violations like fraud, theft, forcible expropriation, enslavement, conquest, looting, murder... (iii) Though I shall not argue it here, as the case I want to make does not depend on it, it is also arguable that Nozick's roughly-Lockean proviso, according to which no one should be made worse off by the appropriation of others relative to some state-of-nature baseline – or else some apparent entitlements cease to be that – is *not* satisfied in a world where very many are both hungry and without access (such as they would have in a state of nature) to as yet unowned land, the possibility of hunting and gathering, and so on.[8]

Now, Nozick is *very* interested in (i) ('a serious matter indeed', 'How *dare* any state or group of individuals...', etc.),[9] but I am interested in this: if his own theory is to be taken seriously at all, we are entitled to be upset about (ii); especially in the light of (iii), but also absolutely. The fact is, however, that when it comes to the question of how to rectify such injustice, Nozick has nothing worthwhile to say. He does not know of a 'theoretically sophisticated' treatment of the problem, he tells us. Then, 'idealizing greatly', he offers some verily abstract, in fact feeble, stuff about putting together historical information concerning past injustices and their effects with probability estimates of what would otherwise have happened. He also suggests that transfer payments according to some patterned principle may – 'perhaps' – be in order *here*, in the matter of rectification, as a 'rough rule of thumb'.[10] Nozick, possessed of a formidably clever mind, exercises it considerably, then, in the argument as to what is and what is not just, but hardly at all over how injustice is to be rectified, saying nothing on this which meets the gravity of the case. His approach to the question is really rather offhand.

This is, it might be said, merely an uninteresting psychological fact, that Nozick is very concerned with the analysis of justice and not so concerned with thinking about the problem of rectification. (After all, no one can take on everything, there must be a division of intellectual labour, and so on.) For my part, I think it not altogether without interest to find, in a writer for whom justice, or entitlement, has an *overriding* status as a value, such a combination of apparently deep concern about the content of it, on the one hand, with so little thought regarding its realization, on the other. But simply to argue for (a conception of) justice, it might again be said, is in its own way to fight for it and so contribute in some measure towards its realization. There is a certain truth in this. But only if the conception of justice argued for stands in some viable relation to the real world. And that is the point here, lifting this issue above the level of mere biographical observation. For it is a structural property of Nozick's particular theory that it cannot be so related to the real world, because of – the very thing he boasts about it – its 'historical' character. This entails that to secure a just world we would need what is impossible, *precise* knowledge of the *precise* historical path to every current property holding, not to speak of accurate estimates of what would or might have occurred, had the myriad violations of individual rights that actually did occur not occurred. (A destitute woman on the streets of New York, whose forebears were enslaved: might she have been, or been married to, a rich West African property owner today... had she still been at all? A wealthy Englishman, staunch supporter of right-wing, so-called libertarian causes: what does his life owe to wealth derived by members of his family from the slave trade?) Nozick, so sensitive of the rights of *each* individual person, is remarkably cavalier with talk about reckoning probabilites or about prospective transfer payments as possible rectifiers. But why should anyone else, particularly coming into the world with (next to) nothing, be willing to be so cavalier? In fact, his theory would only be good, were it not vulnerable to several further objections, for starting the world all over again – which is, of course, also impossible.

This is, consequently, a moralism in the worst sense, a putative morality offered with no concern for 'mere' facts. It seems fair to conclude that it has another, more significant relation to the real world, a latent normative function distinct from its overt one: not the rights and entitlements of each individual person and *therefore* unrestrained libertarian capitalism; unrestrained libertarian capitalism, period. As this, too, may well be unrealizable, the chief ideological function of Nozick's views is probably just to aid governments that most nakedly favour the rich.

I turn now to a type of moral advocacy for which I have a deal more respect. In a well-known article, 'Famine, Affluence, and Morality', Peter Singer makes the following, simple case for an obligation on the part of the affluent to help relieve suffering. 'I begin with the assumption,' he writes, 'that suffering and death from lack of food, shelter, and medical care are bad.' On the basis of this assumption he then argues that 'if it is in our power to prevent something bad from happening, without thereby sacrificing anything of comparable moral importance, we ought, morally, to do it.' Singer also offers a weaker version of the argument (in which 'anything morally significant' is substituted for 'anything of comparable moral importance'), but I shall ignore it as being so weak as to render the argument actually less persuasive: in this form, it would not even oblige you to miss an evening arranged with friends in order to help save someone's life. The example he himself uses in support of his case is of a child drowning in a shallow pond. A passer-by 'ought to wade in and pull the child out'. Deploying argument to the effect that geographical distance from suffering one could help to relieve makes no significant difference to the case, not at any rate in the modern world, and nor does the circumstance that others in a position to help do not do so, Singer arrives at a strong moral obligation for 'people in relatively affluent countries' in face of famine, disease and other such realities outside those countries. The consequences he derives here are stringent ones: such as that people 'ought to give [to famine relief etc.] as much as possible, that is, at least up to the point at which by giving more one would begin to cause serious suffering for oneself and one's dependents'; and 'ought, morally, to be working full time to relieve great suffering of the sort that occurs as a result of famine or other disasters'; and, conversely, ought not to be buying new clothes merely for reasons of fashion.[11]

Brian Barry has subsequently extended the argument into one for humanitarian aid from rich countries to poor at government level. Barry, it is true, speaks in terms of a rather less exacting standard of sacrifice than Singer's but it is not inconsiderable, all the same. 'What, in any case, are we talking about here as the range?' he asks. 'We could perhaps wonder whether the level of aid from a country like the United States should be 3 per cent of GNP (the level of Marshall Aid) or 10 or 25 per cent. But, unless we reject the idea of an obligation to aid those in distress altogether, we can hardly doubt that one quarter of 1 per cent is grotesquely too little.' To this argument from an obligation of 'humanity', he also adds one in the light of a principle of justice, the principle, namely, that 'natural resources are the joint possession of the human race as a whole'. The inhabitants of a country, Barry says, can take no credit for the natural resources it happens to have, nor can they make much of a claim on account of the efforts of their ancestors. From such considerations a second proposal is derived: for 'a tax on the governments of rich countries, assessed as a proportion of gross national product that increases with per capita income, the proceeds to be distributed to poor countries on a parallel basis of negative income tax.'[12]

As I mean to comment critically on the views just expounded, I shall try first to forestall some possible misunderstandings. With one or two reservations which do not affect the general thrust of the case Singer and Barry make, there is a sense in which I accept that case, the moral core of it at least, and the principles of humanity (need) and justice (equality) enunciated by the two of them in making it. There *is* no justification for the polarities of wealth and death, ease and suffering, they refer to and these are a greater blight upon us, the longer they continue in face of the historical possibility of being removed. Some philosophers have criticized the foundation of Singer's case with rights-based arguments of moderating, if not downright conservative, effect, but their criticisms do not strike me as persuasive. They conjure, rather, in my own mind an image I shall call 'The Philosophers at the Feast': of first-world philosophers gathered at a table heavily laden, and discussing with great subtlety what, if anything, they might owe to the starving onlookers. An image, I know, is not a fully reasoned philosophical response but it also has some weight, and to this image there may be added another: of the shock and incomprehension you will sometimes see in the face of a child who has suddenly been confronted for the first time with information about great inhumanity or injustice – a look that something, surely, must be done. This second image encapsulates a better human impulse. In the situation of terrible need and distress that is background to this discussion, anything anyone does towards alleviating it is something important. A statement of moral imperatives and seeking to convince others of them is, accordingly, something important. It is so in so far as it registers a protest; contributes, generally, to sustaining a progressive moral and political culture, or culture of what Herbert Marcuse called 'The Great Refusal'. It is so, too, by virtue of anything it may bring about in the way of material aid or political action, by individuals or governments, that ends up making a material difference for the better here.

It may be added, on Singer's behalf and Barry's, that while speaking in this connection of a need for fundamental changes in moral 'outlook' and 'behaviour', they refer also to the need for concomitant changes in 'way of life', or international institutional framework, in a manner suggesting some appreciation on their part of the far-reaching nature of their own suggestions.[13]

Yet, when all of this has been said, one cannot but be struck by the hopeless abstraction of these arguments: in the sense of their isolating a certain feature of the overall situation from crucial aspects of its context, so generating proposals for practical action that are as good as impossible. I do not say 'of no useful effect'. For, clearly, this kind of advocacy can achieve something, as the efforts of Bob Geldof and the whole Band Aid phenomenon testify. But the disparity between the level of realistically conceivable response to these proposals and the extent of the proposals themselves is, on any scale of measurement, massive. Peter Singer's intended audience is presumably anybody who may happen upon his essay, but he does mention specifically, as a sort of target, teachers and students of philosophy within Western universities.[14] I would not care to estimate how many such have been moved, on reading the essay, to contribute to famine relief nor how much in all they have contributed. But I would be astonished to learn that even one in a hundred of them had contributed up to the level of personal sacrifice that Singer's own argument requires, or indeed anywhere near it. Much the same scepticism can be expressed towards Brian Barry's proposals, in which capitalist governments amongst others and the government of the United States of America amongst them – more prominent this one than any, it seems fair to say, in the effort, often openly murderous, to perpetuate regimes of social inequality across the globe – are envisaged contributing anything up to 25 per cent of GNP in humanitarian aid and then, over and above that, accepting redistributive taxation in favour of poorer countries on grounds of justice. If current aid is, as Barry says, grotesquely too little, these proposals, Singer's and his own, are grotesquely unreal.

It might be said in their defence that they were arguing about what *ought* to be done and not predicting what was likely. A similar consideration applies here, however, as applies in the case of Nozick (though it will be clear by now, I hope, that I do not bracket these writers together in any other respect): this sort of argument has a responsibility, doesn't it?, to take account of worldly facts and what is possible and likely in the light of them. Singer is addressing himself to people in societies in which deep social and economic inequality is a fact, widely accepted as normal; in which the health of many is daily jeopardized and their lives shortened, in the midst of the affluent enjoyments of more fortunate others; in which academic philosophers, not to speak of anyone even better off than they, regularly go to bed at night in warmth and comfort, knowing that others are homeless and even on the streets, but putting it out of their minds; in which some people die of cold in winter; and so forth. That is the structure and the lived experience, and consequently lies deep in the attitudes and the culture, of these societies; bare moral appeals to individual conscience, and for a stringently abstinent life of other-regarding concern, are scarcely any match for it. Barry, for his part, seems able to contemplate as a possibility a system of international justice along the lines set out above, conjoined with any sort of inequality and inequity within the autonomous national units. But here is his own description of the United States, a country obviously critical to any estimate of the realism of his proposal: 'a country... that, in spite of having a quarter of the world's GNP, is unable to provide for much of its population decent medical care, while a substantial proportion live in material conditions of abject squalor that (except for being more dirty and dangerous) recall the cities of Germany and Britain in the aftermath of World War II.'[15] International humanity and justice on the basis of a social order, or rather very many social orders, such as this − is that not a futile abstraction? Do we not have to ask not only what people ought to do but also in what conditions they are likely to recognize that they ought to and likely to want to and be psychologically able to? And to ask what sort of governments, of what sort of societies, would be likely to be swayed by the ethical principles which Barry adduces?

We are driven back here on the need for social revolutions or, in case this way of putting it is preferred, for radical social transformations: in Peter Singer and Brian Barry's putative donor, as well as recipient, countries; involving great changes in moral outlook indeed, but in the indispensable context of fundamental structural change, as is unlikely to be brought about except by organized political movements of some determination and vigour. We are talking, if not necessarily of historical materialism − though, for me, that will do − of an approach to moral issues of more materialist cast at least, more sociologically anchored than this; something else than strenuous but abstract imperatives addressed to a generalized sense of moral obligation.

The upshot, then, is not that ethical analysis and advocacy are unnecessary (as it has been Marxism's traditional weakness to think or, at any rate, *say* that they are), but that they need to be done with some thought for the social and material conditions of attaining any given ideals, the means of and agencies for attaining them, the *social interests and movements* that can conceivably be coupled with or become attached to the ideals and imperatives in question (a need it has been Marxism's traditional strength to understand). Realism in that, and not the cynical, sense is appropriate here and vigorous exhortation not enough. Those socialists who have recently discovered an enthusiasm for discourses and their powers could perhaps get some benefit from reflecting on this.

We might consider, as a relevant current example, South Africa today. The strength of the apartheid state has been shaken recently, and its managers and most of its beneficiaries are acutely concerned about its future and their privileges. As important as exposing the moral iniquities of apartheid has been and will continue to be, and as important as are the solidarity actions that result from this around the world, it is clear that neither the one nor the other has been decisive to what has happened in that country, and nor will they be to the eventual outcome. Decisive has been, and is, the struggle being waged by the black South African masses, an internal agency of social revolution, or radical transformation, constituted by people who know the evils of apartheid *and* have a pressing interest in getting rid of them. Were their struggle to fail or falter, both the extent of the solidarity movement and the volume of moral argument against apartheid would, as likely as not, decrease. At least in one sense, things are no different anywhere else. A decent and humane social order, in which individuals will more generally respond as they should to the needs and the crises of others; a just and egalitarian social order; in a word, socialism – will result from the efforts primarily of those who have a material interest in it, or else it is a dream. The core of that revolutionary force I believe with other Marxists to be the working class, but in the broadest sense: all those – and not just industrial workers – whose labour is exploited for capitalist profit. Socialists who today reject that belief need to come up with an alternative basis for socialism they can show to be more convincing.

I shall conclude by noting what strikes me as an irony in the matter of Marxism's perceived relation to questions of ethics. It is often said that Marxists have a too benign view of human beings, believing them to be intrinsically good. Critics of Marxism, by contrast, are supposedly more hard-headed, because they recognize the less pleasant aspects of human nature and the need to restrain and control these. But is this not a rather one-eyed view of the two sets of assumptions? Marxism certainly looks forward to the possibility of a world in which the grosser forms of violence, cruelty, oppression and so on, have been all but subdued. It does, therefore, suppose that the better and more decent tendencies and modes of behaviour humankind has already widely displayed could eventually come to prevail (by and large, that is, since the notion of a world without *any* human failings or vices is a ridiculous caricature of the Marxist vision). In maintaining, however, that this will only be achievable in a particular kind of social and material context, has not Marxism thereby recognized precisely the other, less happy, more vicious, potentialities and capacities of human beings, the historical weight of these in a record full of suffering and horror, the fact that and the circumstances in which they flourish? Conversely, the appeal by moralists, yesterday and today, to the conscience of the conscientious individual, to his or her sense of duty, of what is right and what is wrong, as though that might suffice to ensure that justice be done or humanity be respected, regardless virtually of the nature of material circumstances; is this not based on a covert assumption that human beings can be treated as if they were *only* conscience and will, each person a simple repository of the good?

Notes

1. Steven Lukes, *Marxism and Morality*, Oxford 1985, pp. 2–4; and documented at pp. 5–25.

2. *Marxism and Morality*, p. 29 – and *passim*.

3. See Norman Geras, 'The Controversy About Marx and Justice', *New Left Review* 150, March/April 1985, pp. 47–85, which includes an extensive bibliography on the debate. The essay is reprinted in my *Literature of Revolution*, Verso, London 1986.

4. Geras, 'The Controversy About Marx and Justice', pp. 81–4.

5. Geras, 'The Controversy About Marx and Justice', pp. 79–81.

6. See, for example, the 'Manifesto of the Communist Party', in Karl Marx

and Frederick Engels, *Collected Works*, London 1975–, Vol. 6, p. 505; and 'On Bakunin's *Statism and Anarchy*', in David McLellan, ed., *Karl Marx: Selected Writings*, Oxford 1977, p. 563.

7. On this, see Norman Geras, *Marx and Human Nature: Refutation of a Legend*, Verso, London 1983.

8. For the proviso, see Robert Nozick, *Anarchy, State, and Utopia*, Oxford 1980, pp. 177–82.

9. *Anarchy, State, and Utopia*, pp. 168, 334.

10. *Anarchy, State, and Utopia*, pp. 152–3, 230–1.

11. Peter Singer, 'Famine, Affluence, and Morality', *Philosophy and Public Affairs* 1, 1971–72, pp. 229–43, at pp. 231–5, 238. The article is reprinted in W. Aiken and H. La Follette, eds., *World Hunger and Moral Obligation*, Englewood Cliffs 1977, and in P. Laslett and J. Fishkin, eds., *Philosophy, Politics and Society* (Fifth Series), Oxford 1979.

12. Brian Barry, 'Humanity and Justice in Global Perspective', in J.R. Pennock and J.W. Chapman, eds., *Nomos XXIV: Ethics, Economics, and the Law*, New York 1982, pp. 219–252, at pp. 225, 237–9, 242.

13. See Singer, 'Famine, Affluence, and Morality', pp. 230, 238; and Barry, 'Humanity and Justice in Global Perspective', pp. 240, 250.

14. 'Famine, Affluence, and Morality', p. 242.

15. 'Humanity and Justice in Global Perspective', pp. 248–9.

2

Our Morals

There were two 'Reigns of Terror', if we would but remember it and consider it; the one wrought murder in hot passion, the other in heartless cold blood; the one lasted mere months, the other had lasted a thousand years.

                                                              Mark Twain

        The restraint of war is the beginning of peace.

                                                         Michael Walzer

In this essay I shall be concerned with what can be termed, broadly, the ethics of revolution. I consider by what normative principles socialists might be guided, whether in judgement or in action, when it comes to revolutionary change. A comprehensive treatment of the issue would require more space than I have here. It would involve not only a theory – be it of needs or of rights or of justice – for the comparative assessment of social and political institutions, a large enough desideratum, evidently, in itself; but also, with it, the resolution of some deep questions in moral philosophy. I shall have some things to say about all this. But I cannot deal with it, so to speak, from the bottom up. In much, I have to proceed instead assertively, relying where I can on the advocacy of others, or on the belief simply that a needed argument could be supplied. The procedure allows me to use what space I have for concentration upon a narrower purpose.

Roughly indicated, this is to argue that socialist discussion of revolutionary ethics (or such of it as is known to me), and the discussion in particular of ends and means, tends to be framed in abstract generalities of a sort which yields neither specific rules or norms of conduct nor much practical guidance for concrete cases; and to suggest that there is a lot to be learned here, by way of trying to repair the deficiency, from another tradition of discourse altogether. The obvious relevance of this other tradition to the moral problems of revolution makes it the more surprising that socialists have drawn so little upon it.

I shall use the term 'revolution' as encompassing at once a standard Marxist and a more limited meaning. That is, I intend by it the overthrow or very radical transformation, within a relatively brief period, of the basic economic and social relations of a society; or of its governing political institutions; or both. The definition is made to cover what are called political, as well as what are called social revolutions. So understood, revolutions need not involve the use of violence. But the problems to be discussed here arise from the fact that they generally do. By 'violence' I shall mean roughly the exercise of physical force so as to kill or injure, inflict direct harm or pain on, human beings. This is in one way narrower, in another broader, than alternative definitions. It is narrower by excluding damage to property; broader because it includes not just that killing, injuring and so on, which is illegal and/or presumed illegitimate, but all such action irrespective of the ends to which it is directed. Whatever may be said in other respects for competing definitions, the one chosen permits a focus on what is most contentious under the rubric of revolutionary means and without foreclosing the moral questions involved.[1]

My discussion is premised on the rejection of two attitudes. One of these is that the use of violence is never justified. The other is that, with regard to political or to revolutionary political violence, no question of justification arises. About the first attitude, I will only say that where it is genuine, held scrupulously, consistently, on pacifist-type grounds, it is a doctrine that would deprive people of all weapons save passive resistance in the face of any oppression or threat, however terrible. If that is not a sufficient case against it, I am unsure what could be. As to the second attitude, this can rest upon a certain kind of Marxist notion about the inevitability or 'immanence' of the ends and the means of socialism; or upon a would-be political realism such as goes back as far at least as Machiavelli. The politicians or soldiers, militants or supporters, of any revolution, it may be said on one or the other basis, will do what they must. All talk of justification, of norms of conduct or ethical appraisal in this area, is idle chatter. No treatment of the ethics of revolution would be serious, in my view, that did not give due weight to considerations of historical realism and to the operation of social determinants and constraints. But these never fully close down the space of political choice and individual decision. To that, moral as well as other standards of judgement are relevant.

I

I begin by providing some necessary context for the problem I wish to address. First, then, people may legitimately revolt against what used commonly to be known as tyranny and is now often termed political oppression. 'The tyranny of established governments,' as it has recently been put, 'gives rise to a right of revolution, held individually by each subject or citizen, rightly exercised by any group of them, of which they cannot be deprived.'[2] This is not a novel nor a specifically socialist thought. It was propounded by, among others, John Locke; who, to the anticipated line of criticism that it was 'destructive to the peace of the world', replied: 'they may as well say, upon the same ground, that honest men may not oppose robbers or pirates, because this may occasion disorder or bloodshed.' The analogy suggests both a notion of revolution as a defensive act and the basis on which it is held to be so and to be therefore justified (when it is). This is the basis – expressed also in the contemporary formulation just cited – of a concept of fundamental rights. As Locke immediately goes on to add regarding robbers and pirates, 'If any mischief come in such cases, it is not to be charged upon him who defends his own right.'[3] Moral justification for revolutionary violence against tyranny, however, does not have to rest on this basis. It can rest equally on a reckoning-up of consequences, on the estimate that the costs in suffering of having to endure arbitrary or oppressive authority are greater than those of destroying it.[4] Irrespective of whether argument about these things is best made by formal appeal to a doctrine of rights, or by such consequentialist judgements, or by some combination of the two, I shall allow myself to speak loosely of a 'right' of revolution wherever revolutionary methods are justified – as they are in the case of tyranny.

Second, there is a right of revolution against grave social injustice: if the basic social relations of any order of society involve that, then a struggle for their expeditious transformation is legitimate. This entails that there is a right of revolution against any *state* which is a bastion against such effort to remove serious, systemic injustice. It entails it but is not equivalent to it. For, conceivably, the state itself might be able to be the instrument of revolutionary transformation. In other terms: where there is a right of social revolution on account of grave injustice there is not necessarily a right of political revolution; but there is one when the state is or becomes a bastion of that injustice.

Many people who call themselves socialists think capitalist societies are marked by grave injustice, and many of these many think also that some of it is systemic rather than incidental injustice. If we are right to think this, those of us who do, then the right of revolution against grave injustice yields a right of revolution against capitalism. Even so, the existence within some capitalist societies of institutions of parliamentary democracy, and of those other legal and civil institutions and norms now typically associated with it, leads to some familiar disagreements about what forms such a revolution might and should take in the societies in question. If, or where, parliamentary-democratic capitalist states are not – or are not necessarily – bastions of capitalist injustice but, as democracies, the possible vehicles of a social revolution against it, there is no need for political revolution and there is no justification for it. But if, on the other hand, even parliamentary-democratic capitalist states, as capitalist states, are such bastions, there is one.[5] I will return to this matter later. It suffices for my main purpose to say that there is a right of revolution against any bastions of capitalist injustice that there are, for there are some.

Note that in resting this right on grave injustice I do not ground it on any claim, such as is sometimes made in this sort of context, that all injustice is itself a kind of violence. Though backed by the threat and periodic use, now more, now less frequent, of violence, there are forms of injustice distinct from it. To put this differently, there are other evils in the world than violence. To argue that (some) violence is justified in a struggle against them, one has no need to extend its core meaning, as given above, to embrace them all. There are here, as Ted Honderich has written, '*two* orders of fact, each of them compelling, each of them terrible'.[6] That order of fact I am calling grave injustice may be formulated, as with tyranny, in terms of a notion of fundamental rights; or in terms of basic needs; or of exploitation; or of equality; or, as is in fact most usual owing to conceptual interdependencies here, of some combination of these. Once more, I set this aside. Capitalist societies, though there are great differences between them, ones that really matter, are gravely unjust on any of these criteria.

There is a right of revolution against tyranny and against any bastion of grave social injustice, including capitalist forms of it. Surveying the contemporary world for examples of these things, we are, unhappily, spoilt for choice. But an example that may be expected to carry the maximum possible number of readers along with the argument that revolution is sometimes justified is South Africa.

Now, what is morally permissible in the pursuit of a just revolutionary struggle? (By a 'just' revolutionary struggle I mean one
to which there is a right, in my loose sense, however that right
is founded as regards bedrock ethical theory.) What can be done,
and what if anything may not be done? Are there limits to the
means that may be used, and what, if so, are they? What are
the broad principles by which we might try to decide them?

I dispose in short order of one kind of answer to these questions.
This is that in any such struggle the means must be prefigurative
of the ends in view. Setting aside some problems about its precise
meaning – for what does a quantity of timber prefigure: a scaffold
or a barn? and what the laying down of weapons: a return of
peace? or impending massacre? – one may concede a value to
some such rough idea. If we can exemplify, can display, our good
ends in the good ways and means we use to achieve them, so
much the better. But in the present context means cannot in
general only reflect the ends in view, because they will also reflect
their own beginnings, so to put it. They are doubly determined:
not only by what they are intended to achieve, the putative goal,
but by that situation which is their starting point as well. It is
in the nature of the problem under discussion – of revolution
– that this starting point has ugly features, including the mobilization of violence on its behalf. How could the means of opposing
it not reflect some of that ugliness; how, even in trying to prefigure
a better future, avoid being scarred by an awful past? Shooting
at the direct agents of a hated tyranny is still killing people; it
is a state of war and, as such, not 'prefigurative' of human harmony
or even of reasonably tolerable social order, though it may be
necessary in order to achieve that. To point this out is just to
insist on an indispensable minimum of realism. All the same, it
may then be said, revolutionary means must at least prefigure
their intended ends to some, large extent. But to what extent?
Which non-prefigurative means, if one is going to speak in this
way, may, and which if any may not, be used in a just revolutionary
struggle? The notion of prefiguration gives no determinate answer
to our question, merely another (and in my view unhelpful) lan-

guage in which to formulate it.[7]

Let us see, then, if there is guidance to be had from what is perhaps the dominant form of argument in socialist discussions of revolution, and in the literature on justifications for political violence more generally. I refer to argument of a consequentialist kind concerning the costs and benefits of projected or anticipated violence relative to those of a continuation of the status quo. In the words of one writer, we can make 'rough consequentialist calculations' in the following spirit: 'revolutionary violence is only justified when, of the alternatives available, it will, everything considered, make for less misery and human degradation all around.' The common idea he so expresses is of what Barrington Moore has called a 'calculus of suffering'.[8] It should be noted, however, that consequentialist judgement in this connection does not have to rest, as these formulations suggest it at least might, on some form of philosophical utilitarianism. It need not be unified by reliance on the single measure of suffering/happiness. It could take a more pluralistic form, with the use of a number of indices (happiness/welfare *and*, say, freedom, or equality) not thought reducible one to another.[9] There is even possible here what I shall term a consequentialism of rights: that is to say, a view that there are basic rights, worth fighting for when infringed, but under a restriction of 'proportionality'; such as would oblige one to compare violations of rights likely to result from the fighting with 'those it intends to rectify'.[10]

Assume, anyway, that the sort of rough calculation envisaged points to a revolutionary struggle being justified. Then at least theoretically, two kinds of limit on the choice of means would seem to be derivable from these forms of reasoning, a qualitative and a quantitative one. It is not the case that anything whatsoever could be shown to be – though, of course, anything could be *said* to be – legitimate in a just revolutionary cause on the basis of consequentialist reasoning. For, first, the means chosen must be apt. They must be efficacious means (by which I do not mean they must be guaranteed of success, merely able in principle to achieve the projected end; every revolution runs some significant risk of defeat). As the point was put by Trotsky in a well-known discussion of these issues: 'That is permissible ... which *really* leads to the liberation of mankind', and 'Precisely from this it flows that *not* all means are permissible.'[11] Not anything, in other words, could work. Second, it is in the nature of the approach we are presently considering that from a range of alternative means all judged to be efficacious in principle, those that are least costly, by the indices of cost thought to matter, must be chosen. This would presumably exclude unnecessary or excessive violence: that is, all violence surplus to what is needed to win the struggle, even if such surplus violence would leave a balance in favour of revolution in the overall calculation. We have, then, a requirement of efficacy, with the attached proviso of minimum necessary force. If we now ask, however, what in particular is allowed and what ruled out by these two principles, or even what kinds of action or policy are permitted and excluded, the answer is far from clear. As Trotsky himself says in the same place: 'These criteria do not, of course, give a ready answer to the question as to what is permissible and what is not permissible in each separate case. ... Problems of revolutionary morality are fused with the problems of revolutionary strategy and tactics.'

But we must press the question, for we need more than this. That one's means should be efficacious and no more violent than necessary is, as a code of revolutionary ethics, a bit thin. So: what in particular, what in the way specifically of violence and its various forms, might be excluded by the two principles? Within the broad consequentialist framework we are exploring, there are in fact, if no precise answers here, at least responses in contrasting spirit. One of them is Trotsky's own: namely, that not very much can be excluded. Another is that some things – surely – must be. As to the first, Trotsky is quite forthright about it: 'the warring classes will seek to gain victory *by every means*.'[12] We may take it he does not intend by this to contradict his own emphatic statement that not all means are allowed; that he intends only that, beyond the requirement of their being efficacious for the end of liberation, the means of revolution cannot be further morally constrained. He is, at any rate, consistent in using formulations to the effect that the revolutionary class struggle is, or is always likely to become, a form of total war in which conventional moral limits go by the board. Thus he writes, 'The highest form of the class struggle is civil war which explodes into mid-air all moral ties between the hostile classes'; and 'To attempt to subordinate it to abstract "norms" means in fact to disarm the workers in the face of an enemy armed to the teeth.' The workers, Trotsky says further, must be free from the 'fiction' of 'transcendental morality'. His view, it will be evident, is harmonious with a famous formula of Lenin's about the dictatorship of the proletariat: 'The revolutionary dictatorship of the proletariat is rule won and maintained by the use of violence by the proletariat against the bourgeoisie, rule that is unrestricted by any laws.'[13]

In other socialist writing there has been a different inflection: even from within the overall consequentialist approach, a concern to uphold at least some general moral prohibitions. What is most illuminating about it, however, is the ambiguity of the terms in which it is typically expressed. Herbert Marcuse, for example, defending the rationality of historical judgement concerning the likely all-round effects of any revolution for human freedom and happiness, insists nevertheless on the unimpaired validity of certain 'general norms'. No matter how rationally one might justify revolutionary means by such historical reckoning, he says, 'there are forms of violence and suppression which no revolutionary situation can justify because they negate the very end for which the revolution is a means.' He mentions specifically in this connection 'cruelty, and indiscriminate terror'. Anthony Arblaster argues similarly. He affirms, following Trotsky, that the principle of efficacy (that the means chosen must 'really' be means to the end in view) will disqualify some putative means; and equally that this does not take us very far as a guide to action. Still, there are means, he holds, that so 'contradict' the ends of liberation that they must be ruled out for the Left. He mentions specifically 'cruelty or torture'.

The question here is what precisely the point is of saying that means such as these 'negate' or 'contradict' the given end. Is it that they could not contribute to its achievement? Or that they are 'never justified, however admirable the end they may actually advance'?[14] Are they disqualified because they could not work? Or even if they could? If the first, then we do not have a separate consideration from that of efficacy. We have no restriction upon the exercise of consequentialist calculation. One is bound to ask, therefore, why just these means – cruelty, terror, torture – are picked out by name for exclusion. Why could they not simply be reckoned up with everything else? If they were never efficacious in a just cause, that would ensure their exclusion. One gets the strong sense here of a worry lest this kind of reckoning should sometimes yield the wrong result, lest these means might turn out in some circumstances to be efficacious even in a just cause; and of an impulse, consequently, to put them beyond calculation. So they should be put. But placed as we are in this case before the second of the two possibilities, that these means are to be disqualified, then, irrespective of considerations of efficacy, we are bound to pose another question. Why should consequentialist calculation stop precisely here and not earlier or elsewhere, with other forms of violence? Why are just these the limits? If it is said, because the means in question are especially horrible, indeed they are. But neither of the writers whose views we are considering would be (or have been) willing to say that those forms of violence justifiable within a legitimate revolutionary struggle – killing, for example, or maiming by trying but failing to kill – are not horrible at all. So, by what criteria are we to say when horrible means have become too horrible to countenance?

There is insufficient determinacy in the positions we have had before us up to now. They give us only the most general of notions, whether about efficacy and the weighing of consequences or about some hypothetical but unexplained limits to this. General notions, to be sure, are better than nothing. But if they are too general to yield any more precise guidance, they may well come to nothing under the pressures of revolutionary conflict. Trotsky's approach states clearly one of the logics of a just revolutionary struggle:

the moral importance of winning. What matters is what will succeed, and the indeterminacy lies in it being hard to say in the
abstract what will. The other approach states another logic, that
there must surely be moral limits of some kind to what could
be justified, even in order to win. But it states it unclearly; its
indeterminacy lies in the difficulty of defining where such limits
fall and why. Some effort of definition is, however, indispensable.

To appreciate more fully the need for it, one has only to reflect
a moment on some typical circumstances of revolution. First, if
it has indeed come to revolution, then an enormous amount is
at stake. For, as not only Marx but also Locke pointed out, and
contrary to a myth common with more vulgar forms of conserva-
tism, revolutions are not easily stirred up.[15] Where it has come
to a revolutionary struggle, the regime or order – the situation
– against which this is directed is generally not just bad but terrible:
whether in terms of basic rights, of misery and suffering, or other
indices of human cost. And this is to say nothing about such further,
often frightful, costs as may be imposed, in the event of a defeat,
by the opponents of revolution. Second, and as nearly all theoretical reflection on political violence unites in emphasizing, against
this backdrop there are also very large uncertainties. Which means
will be efficacious and which not and which be counter-productive?
What violence is necessary to the goals of revolution and what
violence excessive? In general, how much confidence can there
be in judgements about these matters made under great pressure?
Two overarching questions may serve to organize the whole range
here. Given what is likely to be at stake, can a revolutionary
movement afford to forswear in advance the use of any means
from which it might conceivably derive advantage? On the other
hand, given the uncertainties, in what ways, and how far, may
it legitimately by its actions put the lives or persons of others
in jeopardy, how far contravene the general moral rules or norms
which serve (when they do serve) to protect these?

The issues are extremely difficult. We need clearer lines. As
one more way of bringing this into focus, the difficulty and the
need alike, I want now to consider some arguments in Steven

Lukes's recent, widely noticed critique of the moral record of Marxism. The latter, according to Lukes, 'has from its beginning exhibited a certain approach to moral questions that has disabled it from offering moral resistance to measures taken in its name.' Having no satisfactory account of justice and rights; concerned, as a form of long-range consequentialism, with optimal outcomes rather than 'agent-centred restrictions'; morally blind, in the pursuit of large emancipatory goals, to the present interests of living persons; Marxism could not deal adequately with 'injustice, violations of rights ... the resort to impermissible means'. It 'has never come properly to grips with the means–ends issue, and the problem of dirty hands.' I find much to quarrel with in the balance of Lukes's account but I shall pass over it, as some of the necessary critical points have already been well made by others. The problem of means and ends and ruthless solutions to it are not weaknesses special to Marxism, nor is subordinating the interests of living persons to a projected larger good or goal; they seem nicely distributed across the political spectrum. Many of the Marxist texts Lukes cites in support of his case evince a greater awareness of the complexity of these matters than he allows.[16] There is in the present context a more important thing to be pursued. Lukes makes a valid point, one which Marxists – amongst others – ought to digest. But it is vitiated by the fact that he does not face up squarely either to the kind of background against which the questions here at issue arise or to the difficulty of proposing definite answers to them.

Marxist discussion of ends and means has been deficient; that is true. As was part of my purpose to illustrate in what has gone before, it has not produced an adequately determinate code of revolutionary ethics or conduct. It is also the case, as I go on to argue, that remedying this deficiency must mean giving weight to 'agent-centred restrictions': to individual rights. To the extent that Marxists have often been wary of or hostile to concepts of rights, they have not been well-placed to resolve these issues satisfactorily. Lukes's book valuably draws attention to this. The difficulty it fails to address is that of how far the oppressed are morally obliged to respect the rights of their oppressors. May slaves not kill their masters or overseers, or wound them in attempting to escape? May they tear them limb from limb? Or only seek to overpower them? Or what? There are rights – to life, against personal violation, and so on – involved here. How far must the victims and opponents of an unjust or tyrannical regime respect the rights of its defenders, supporters, beneficiaries? There is not an unlimited range of answers to this sort of question. We may take it, from the whole spirit of Lukes's approach, that he would not say these rights should be set at naught. The gross alternatives remaining are, then, to treat them as absolute, inviolable in all circumstances, or to give them some weight. Again, I discount the first of these alternatives: it appears clear from much that Lukes says that to put forward a variety of socialist pacifism is not his intention. The rights, therefore, even of oppressors, even of the defenders, supporters, beneficiaries, of injustice or tyranny, are to be given some weight.

How much? Which rights, all or only some of them, and what sort of weight? A general emphasis upon individual rights is, I have already said, of value in this context. But as an answer to the real problems posed by revolution, it is, in *so* general, so indeterminate a form, not only not better than the kind of consequentialism Lukes criticizes, it may turn out in practice to be no different from it. For, if all we can say is that (some?) rights must be taken seriously or more seriously than a lot of Marxists have been disposed to take them, that they must be given some or even a lot of weight, they are thereby in effect just thrown in with all other considerations, thrown into some overall calculation or comparison or judgement. When very much is at stake, in situations of dire pressure, they may not then count for enough, the broad emphasis on their importance notwithstanding. The point may be made clearer by adverting once more to Trotsky's contention that revolution comes down to a form of war and as such cannot be constrained by general or transcendental moral norms. Now, actually, revolution is not always or at once generalized war. Still, the relation between it, civil war and wider warfare has been close enough historically to highlight the obvious point that revolutions typically involve the most intense conflicts; conflicts as must make at least some rights and what they protect forfeit. Set against this background, there is nothing whatever specifically Marxist about Trotsky's reasoning. On the contrary, as Michael Walzer has written in a work systematically critical of such reasoning: 'Either fight all-out or not at all. This argument is often said to be typical of American [!] thought, but in fact it is universal in the history of war.'

Trotsky's view has, I believe, to be rejected. But we are better placed to reject it if we recognize it for what it is, not some specially Marxist form of ruthlessness, but an argument about human warfare which politicians and generals of every stripe have been known to voice: that 'for the sake of the cause', 'for justice', because of 'the moral urgency of victory', one must fight without restraint.[17] And we are better placed to reject it if we recognize also that where rights and lives and life chances are in general jeopardy, whether owing to war or to revolution or to those circumstances that make revolution justifiable, there general affirmations of the importance of rights are insufficient, as insufficient as the plea for prefigurative forms of struggle; more precise discriminations are required. The second recognition follows close upon the first.

It is for the same reason as I find Lukes's argument insufficient that I am unhappy also with the conclusion drawn by Kate Soper in the otherwise pertinent criticisms of it to which I have already once made reference. She too finds the bare appeal to 'respect for the principle of individual rights' inadequate. But she goes on to conclude, in a way quite as indeterminate as Lukes's own, that 'no absolute rule applies'; that 'all situations requiring moral decision are concrete and have to be judged on their merits'; that to act morally is 'to act in the light of general rules', but sometimes also 'in contradiction with one or other' of them. As she says further: 'I am put in mind here of E.P. Thompson's recommendation that humanist attitudes should find expression "whenever and to the degree that contingencies allow", and of his come-back to his exasperated critics: "what else can one say?

That they must always find expression irrespective of contingencies?" The argument seems clumsy, somehow unsatisfactory – yet in essence I think it is the right one. On the other hand, the morality it implies is not easy to formulate or render into a coherent whole, since it requires us to combine respect for the individual with an agreement to waive that respect in certain conditions.'[18]

Whatever might be said about this as a general observation on the nature of moral choice, for the sort of circumstances to which we here must apply it I think it is, and not merely seems, unsatisfactory. 'To the degree that contingencies allow': that is not a happy formula for a socialist or revolutionary ethic. Nor is: agreement to waive respect for the individual 'in certain conditions'. It is all too easy to envisage either of them as a recipe for complete moral cynicism. Of course, this is not the spirit in which Soper intends them; the very opposite. Even so, neither formula is helpful. By their nature they do nothing at all to delimit the ways in which, or the extent to which, 'contingencies' and 'conditions' may be permitted to displace 'general rules'. If such rules do not themselves incorporate at least the more likely, the more easily foreseeable, conditions and contingencies, then they are no good.

We only need to think about how these formulations, as well as all the others earlier reviewed, might bear upon a concrete case, to be brought face to face with their limitations. The South African state today is for the large majority of those subject to it a vicious tyranny. It is a bastion of grave injustice if such there be. The black people of that country are deprived of the most elementary political rights, and the violence mobilized against them, well documented, widely broadcast – sjambok-wielding police violence and then more deadly than that; an epidemic of torture; 'accidental' death in police custody; one of the highest rates of judicial execution in the world, its victims nearly all black; Latin American style 'disappearances', the kidnapping and murder of chosen individuals by freelance death squads with who knows what degree of connivance and participation by the 'security' services of the state – this violence stands between an entire people and its goal of a more just and happier condition. That a counter-violence of opposition to such a regime could not be justified, because political violence in general cannot ever be, is a view I have already rejected. Here then, in turn, are some of the kinds of thing that occurred in South Africa during 1985 and 1986, years of a great wave of black resistance and struggle, before these were set back by the imposition of a state of emergency in June of the latter year. Bombs were placed in or near police stations, in the offices of the South African Defence Force, in one case in a shopping centre; the explosions caused death and injury. Black policemen and town councillors were attacked and killed. So were suspected police informers and collaborators, and individuals buying from certain shops in violation of a campaign of economic boycott. Sometimes such people were attacked in their homes and members of their families harmed. Often they were killed in shockingly brutal ways. 'One particularly cruel form of killing, known as the necklace, is to put a burning tyre around the neck of a victim who then dies a slow and painful death.'[19]

Now, how could we discriminate, on the basis of what we have from this discussion so far, of the putative ethic of revolution any of it might be thought to define, as to the legitimacy or otherwise of these several actions? Even if, as I suspect is likely, it may be said here that it is not for *us* so to discriminate, because it is not our struggle – a view I shall in due course also reject – still, how then could the participants in that struggle, or the leaders of it, discriminate? How much would it help anyone to be told that the means of struggle must 'really' be means to the liberation of the majority of South Africans, or must not too obviously 'negate' or 'contradict' that end, or must take some significant account of individual rights, or must respect these to the degree that 'contingencies' allow, or must only waive them 'in certain conditions'? In truth, it would help them precious little; for all that some of these arguments do have a value as very general guidelines. The socialist discussion of ends and means is wanting in specificity. We need to look elsewhere.

36

II

Where I shall suggest we need to look is by now perhaps obvious. It is to the theory and practice of war: more specifically, to just war doctrine and, via that, to some of the rules of actual warfare. I introduce the topic on a semi-personal note. My own reason initially for looking to this material, what I sought there, and what on the other hand I found, are two different things. For, what I sought in starting to think again in a general way about the ethics of revolution were the considerations typically adduced to legitimate war, the commonest grounds for war being qualified as 'just'. I sought them as a way of focusing on the weakness in political viewpoints – some kinds of contemporary liberalism, most kinds of conservatism – generally hostile to revolution, yet at the same time more than willing to countenance the moral necessity, in certain circumstances, of war. In the event, that turns out to be light work. If war is sometimes justified, then so too is revolution, the reasons given on their behalf being of a kind: self-defence, autonomy, rights and freedoms, the throwing off of an oppressor, and so forth. All of this falls under the heading, one side of a distinction which is central in the literature, of *jus ad bellum*: the justice *of* war. What I found, however, not in the sense of having been altogether unaware of it before, but in the sense of coming to realize here was matter germane to the problems of socialist ethics and yet not much brought to bear upon them – what I found was the other side of the same distinction, namely *jus in bello*, justice *in* war: a body of doctrine concerning the methods of legitimate warfare, whether or not in a just cause; rules applicable to both parties; the obligation to fight even against aggression within certain moral limits.[20]

The most striking feature of this literature and indeed domain, coming at it from the angle we here do, is the contrast between the relative poverty, the underdevelopment, of socialist principles for revolutionary conduct, and the wealth of the rules of war, the fullness and determinacy of *jus in bello*. The number, the detail and the complexity of these rules, and of the qualifications to them, do stand out in the comparison. There are rules about combatant and non-combatant status, about the wounded and those rendered helpless in combat, about giving quarter to surrendering soldiers. There are rules defining the rights and obligations of prisoners of war, and concerning warfare at sea, and about the conduct of sieges. There are rules defining rights of neutrality and rules about partisan warfare. There are prohibitions on certain kinds of weapons. And so on. Such a list is in fact but a poor indication of the extent of the contrast: on one side, only the vaguest of notions; on the other, a vast and detailed literature, not to speak of well-developed international codes and conventions.

Now, it may be said that all these rules are much violated in the course of real war and so they are. But the point is that there exist, nevertheless, definite rules and that they are observed often enough to be of value. It is not difficult, again, to speculate on some possible reasons for the contrast. Wars are fought in the main between states and though states clearly have an interest in breaking the rules of war, otherwise they would do less of this than they in fact do, there must be enough of a common interest among them in having codes of rules for these to have evolved to the point they have. Few states, however, if any, can have an interest in drawing up, much less in observing, a comparable code of rules to govern possible revolutionary struggles against them. Oppressive regimes, it may therefore also be said, will use – do use, across the globe – the most savage forms of violence in the counter-revolutionary cause: use terror, torture, massacre. But those are *their* crimes. They are their morals; they cannot be ours. Whatever the interests of any state may be, there are reasons why a socialist ethic of revolution must embody a precise code of moral limits and moral rules.

Within the multiplicity of rules that apply to the waging of war, two principal types are relevant in the present context. One of them concerns the category of persons at whom violence may be directed: those who are legitimate targets of attack, who may be killed. The other concerns the manner of attack: how or in what circumstances they may be killed.[21] I shall consider each type in turn with a view to its bearing upon our subject.

Rules of the first sort draw a distinction between combatants and non-combatants. Under the concept of non-combatant immunity, they delineate a large area – the many people – off limits to any violent attack. In the context of war, this distinction, very roughly, is between soldiers on the one hand, and 'innocent' civilians on the other. It is important, however, that the notion of innocence involved in it is a special one. It has nothing to do with judgements of moral culpability. The soldier may be a reluctant conscript and the civilian an avid supporter of the war, even contributing time and effort to sustaining or boosting a war-fighting morale. The point is only that soldiers constitute, have made themselves or been made by others into, a threat. As, literally, the warriors of one or other side, those directly making war and so putting lives and persons in jeopardy, they are legitimately subject to violence themselves. There is an analogy with a justified act of self-defence outside of war: one may use deadly force against somebody threatening one's life if that is the only possibility of escape, irrespective of the attacker's motives or moral character, of whether or not he or she was egged on by others, and so on. Also important here is the circumstance that, as with many such distinctions, where the line falls exactly may be a difficult matter, a matter of some contention; the crucial thing is that there is a line. As Dr Johnson said, apparently: 'the fact of twilight does not mean you cannot tell day from night.' So, in modern war the category of combatant has been extended to include munitions workers (but only as engaged in, when at their place of, work). It does not, however, include workers processing soldiers' rations. Manufacturing their weaponry counts as a contribution to the threat, while making what they need simply as human beings does not.[22]

Applying this now to the case of a regime against which, on account of tyranny or injustice, there is a right of revolution, the distinction must be made between its direct agents of oppression and everybody else. Here again there are likely to be difficult and contentious borderline instances. But the boundary needs to be quite narrowly drawn which defines such a regime's combatants. They are its leaders, soldiers, police, security agents, jailers, torturers; in general, those warring on its behalf, those involved in imposing and enforcing oppressive laws.[23] That would include, as in the South African case, known police informers and collaborators (a matter to which I return), but would not, without more ado, include just every kind of state employee; teachers, say, or health workers. And it would not include, either, the civilian population at large, even such sectors of this as may be open supporters or beneficiaries of the regime in question. If it is said here that political supporters or economic beneficiaries of an oppressive regime are *ipso facto* the enemies of its victims and therefore legitimate targets of revolutionary violence, it may be noted simply, in anticipation of the argument I later make against this, that much the same could be said about the civilians of an enemy power in time of war – in order to justify massacring them. It is a line of thought, of justification and of action that certainly occurs in war, but one also, I presume, that would give most socialists pause.

In its struggle for the liberation of Guiné from colonial rule, the PAIGC made a distinction between 'the Portuguese people ... Portuguese individuals or families' and 'Portuguese colonialism': it was fighting, it said, against the latter and not the former. In the South African context there are public statements also from the ANC to the effect that the targets of its armed struggle are police and military ones; not civilians.[24] These discriminations agree with a 'political code ... roughly analogous to the laws of war', one less respected, according to Michael Walzer, in our own century than in the last.[25] But it is a code, in any case, which many of us – overtly or not, some of us perhaps only half-consciously – refer to or make use of in a rough and ready way in thinking about these matters, and whether we are fully aware or not of the military analogy. It is a better instrument for the assessment of putatively revolutionary means than the various formulae I began by reviewing. It enables us to say, for example, that setting bombs against military and police personnel or installations is, where there is a right of revolution, a legitimate means of it, while bombing supermarkets or shopping centres, restaurants and other such venues is not. To be precise here: doing this is not, or is not only, a 'mistake', tactically, politically. It is a moral wrong, a crime. So clearly, according to a principle of non-combatant immunity adapted to the revolutionary setting, are the taking and killing of innocent hostages; making targets of people because of their country of origin, or of the airline they are travelling with, or of their destination; or because they are bourgeois, or are captains of industry, or settlers, or members of a particular ethnic group. So, generally, is terrorism in the true sense: the use of more or less random violence against whole populations. It is clearer to say of this, of indiscriminate terror, that it is wrong because it is making war on people who are not themselves making war, than that it negates the ends of revolution.

Trotsky, in *Their Morals and Ours*, mocks the distinction I here uphold; for his part defending, with reference to Bolshevik policy during the Russian civil war, the practice of taking hostages. The arguments behind the mockery, however, blur two significant points. Civil war, he contends, as the most severe of all forms of war, 'is unthinkable not only without violence against tertiary figures but, under contemporary technique, without killing old men, old women and children.' The difference between shooting soldiers at the front and shooting hostages, between open battle and 'the seizure of non-participants', he dismisses as 'a wretched and stupid evasion': many participants are just duped or unwilling conscripts; the means of modern war inevitably kill thousands of non-participants; those taken as hostages 'are at least bound by ties of class and family solidarity with one of the camps, or with the leaders of that camp.'[26] The first thing wrong with these arguments has already been spoken of. Because many who fight are blameless, more or less, for the war in which they fight, the boundary around the legitimate targets of war is quickly – massively – relaxed, to take in very large numbers of people whose existence and activities are not directly menacing. Innocence in one sense legitimates the deliberate killing of innocents in another. Trotsky's point is made in connection specifically with the practice of hostage taking. The formula, however, 'ties of class and family solidarity', is one, imaginably, of even larger-scale horror. It is an awful one.

Secondly, under the heading of 'contemporary technique', Trotsky too easily elides the difference between deliberately killing or injuring non-combatants and doing so unintentionally, even if as an effect of one's intended ends. I have not the space adequately to examine the principle normally adduced here, namely that of 'double effect', nor such related notions as 'collateral damage'. They give us no easy solutions anyway; can be, and are often abused. All the same, there is a line, a difficult one once more, which Trotsky's way of speaking casually dissolves. The principle of double effect, briefly and incompletely stated, permits an act likely to have some evil consequences, provided that these evils are not part of one's ends, nor means to one's ends; and – on an interpretation of the principle which I am persuaded of – provided also that one seeks to minimize the likely evils or the risk of them, at some cost to oneself.[27] In war, bombing an important military target with the foreseeable side effect of limited civilian casualties (against some rather rough notion of proportionality), this is one thing; bombing whole cities in order to kill and terrorize civilians and so break their morale is another. So too, arguably, in the sphere of revolutionary struggle, is bombing or burning the home of a police or other official, and (members of) his or her family with it.

A sense of proportion will not come amiss as regards the nature of Trotsky's argument and the policies it defends. I say this not in order backhandedly to condone the view I have just criticized, merely as a necessary point in these times about Marxism's place in the world. The argument and the policies tell against Trotsky and the Bolsheviks – just as equally brutal arguments and, in cost of lives, worse measures tell against such statesmen of the liberal democracies as Winston Churchill and Harry Truman. There is a hard matter here. But it is about politics and war much more than it is about Marxism.[28]

I turn now to rules of the second kind: concerning legitimate modes of attack; setting limits to how those who are properly targets in war may be killed. The basis of these rules, it must be said, is rather less obvious. It may even be the case that the particular prohibitions obtaining at any time against this or that sort of weapon have no other foundation than the formal conventions agreed amongst states. There is a principle, nevertheless, which seems to inform at least some of them and which is of relevance and value in the revolutionary setting. It can be expressed in one way as a notion of minimum force: one's weapons must be capable of stopping enemy combatants, which in the given circumstances involves killing them; but they should not, beyond this, seek gratuitously to accentuate suffering. The same thing can be expressed another way, in a formulation I have adapted from Thomas Nagel, by saying that the weapons should attack the combatant and not the person. They should not, therefore, be 'designed to maim or disfigure or torture' him or her.[29] Here again I think we have a clearer reason for ruling out 'particularly cruel' weapons and, more generally, cruel methods of killing, the deliberate infliction and aggravation of pain, as in torture, than if we say that these contradict the ends of liberation. Just as only the combatants of the other side may be attacked, because they are the ones making war on you, so too they may be 'stopped', killed, because that puts an end to the threat they have been to you or their contribution to it. Extreme and purposeful cruelty, beyond what is necessarily involved in any act of killing or wounding, is wrong because it is more than their activities can justify – as it were defensively – on your own part. Unless, that is, it is allowed that the ethics of socialism may embody, as a component, some fairly terrible theory of retributive punishment. I assume without argument here that they may not.

A slow, painful death by burning, consequently, lies beyond the limits of what is morally defensible in the light of an ethic of just revolutionary struggle. Likewise, killing an old woman by forcing her to drink the bottle of detergent or cooking oil she

has bought in defiance of a shop boycott. (I leave aside the question
of whether this defiance can be taken to make of her an agent
of oppression, as I think it cannot. For, there are, anyway, forms
of community pressure appropriate to meeting the specific nature
of the threat she represents, her challenge to a boycott. This con-
temptuous cruelty far exceeds them.[30]) *Jus ad bellum* is in itself
no guarantee of *jus in bello*. The justice of the cause does not
make good, cannot transmute, moral atrocities committed in its
name. In the case of South Africa, here chosen to exemplify these
issues precisely because of the overwhelming justice of the revolutionary cause, the briefest description of certain episodes of violence suffices to communicate a sense of something in them other
than the legitimate concerns of a just revolutionary struggle.

> They chased her across the veld, they beat her, they stoned her,
> they tore her clothes off, they set her on fire, they put a huge rock
> on her so that she couldn't get up and they rammed a broken bottle
> into her vagina.

> As the family cowered in the house, they saw the eldest son, who
> ran for help grabbed by the mob and dismembered in the street.
> As the mob burst into the house, [he] shot his younger son in the
> head to save him from a similar fate.[31]

At this point I anticipate two types of counsel: one, of historical
realism; the other, to speak not of what does not concern you.
There is more to be said for the first but I address myself to
both. In any historically, or sociologically – or just 'humanly' –
informed perspective, there must be an acknowledgement of some
limits to the proper reach of moral discourse itself. To let an
extreme case illustrate this: if a group of slaves or of prisoners
in a concentration camp should, having the opportunity, suddenly
get the better of a vicious overseer or guard and brutally slaughter
him, it would not be apt to say they had gone too far or to reflect
critically on the notion of 'cruel or unusual' punishments. *In extre-*

mis, moral judgement fails. More generally, the violence of oppressors tends to breed violence amongst those they oppress. Their brutalities are brutalizing. A political or social order that must be overthrown by revolution will have generated, not only amongst its defenders but also with some of its victims, impulses of moral criminality and murderousness. An altogether morally 'clean' revolutionary struggle is probably rare, therefore, if it is conceivable. Even so, two points need to be emphasized about this.

First, the plea of *in extremis* is just that. It cannot too quickly or easily accommodate every horror generated out of situations of conflict. A young, defenceless woman (subject of the first description above), merely rumoured to be a police agent and perhaps not one, is not a sadistic concentration camp guard. The *son* of a collaborating official (subject of the second description) is not a ruthless slave-driver. Second, even if the perspective of historical realism may make certain occurrences understandable, it does not make them right. It does not make them right, in particular, in the perspective – as important this one as the other – of revolutionary policy and morality. The leaders, the militants, of a movement against injustice are obliged for their part to try, so far as it is in their power, to bring a disciplined, scrupulous, discriminating, ethical code into the dark history they are fighting to transform. Where understanding, on the one hand, and moral discrimination, on the other – or historical explanation and political choice; or sociological realism and the responsibility of individuals and movements for what they do – where these two meet, come face to face, there is a difficult philosophical issue indeed. Except, however, for the most extreme of determinisms, the first cannot altogether relieve the second of its burdens.

Only the discipline and scruple, incidentally, self-imposed by a revolutionary movement in the light of a defensible code of ethical principles and constraints, can serve to mitigate a problem just alluded to and which, as far as I can see, has no genuinely satisfactory solution. This is that, in the context of a just revolutionary struggle, some of those rightly to be regarded as the combatants

of tyranny or injustice will not be identified, as others of them
are, by uniforms, insignia and the like, and will take some care
not to be identified at all. At the same time the possibilities of
sound judicial methods for establishing that they are informers,
collaborators, agents or what have you, are either limited or non-
existent. The danger of individuals being wrongly accused and
killed are great. These dangers will be the more severe, obviously,
as will be the chances of people resorting to violence to settle
a personal score or for some other repugnant motive, if it is the
anger of more or less spontaneously formed crowds and not any
procedures informed by care or principle that determine an individual's fate.

As for the other counsel, against making judgements from outside on the struggles of others, what can be conceded to it, it
seems to me, is only that opinion in these circumstances should
not be hasty, but considered. Taken strictly, however, it is an
admonition that would have forbidden Western socialists in the
1930s from expressing any criticism of the crimes of Stalin; or,
more recently, would have excluded adverse comment upon those
of Pol Pot and the Khmer Rouge. It is not a counsel to be heeded.
Reflection on the Stalinist example reveals its effective meaning.
For, it was doubtless one consideration in persuading many Western communists and socialists to maintain an uncritical, apologetic,
attitude to Stalinist policies and practices which they ought to
have condemned. It is a counsel, in fact, to refrain not from judgement as such but only from critical judgement.

Let us make explicit, then, the normative basis of the foregoing
argument for extending central notions in just war doctrine to
the case of revolutionary struggle. This basis is a principle that
individuals have rights – against being killed or violated – rights
that may not, in general, be set aside; unless they forfeit them
by making war themselves in defence of tyranny or grave injustice.
Here, I shall simply ignore the rather large question of whether
such rights are the proper axiomatic starting point for an adequate
moral doctrine or whether they are, rather, to be derived from
other premisses. I bypass this question in a vulgar, practical man-

ner. They are important for us one way or another: as axiomatic values; or because socialists generally profess a respect for human life and well-being, and rights are a crucial way of embodying that respect, of giving it normative or regulative force against this or that exigency or passion of the moment. As the point was expressed by Victor Serge, a point, in his view, to 'take precedence before all tactical considerations': *'Defence of man. Respect for man. Man must be given his rights, his security, his value. Without these, there is no Socialism. Without these all is false, bankrupt and spoiled. I mean: man whoever he is, be he the meanest of men − "class-enemy", son or grandson of a bourgeois, I do not care. It must never be forgotten that a human being is a human being.'*[32]

This is a necessary sensibility, that must inform every genuine struggle against oppression or injustice. In the circumstances and under the pressures of revolution, as of war, it can only be made effective at all if the conditions in which, and the extent to which the relevant rights may be forfeit are spelled out within very tight limitation. This must mean in an 'individualized' way. Otherwise, the rights, as individual rights, are not worth a fig. Whatever problems there may be, for example, in setting boundaries around the category of 'combatant', the principle from just war theory that 'no one can be forced to fight or to risk [their] life, no one can be threatened with war or warred against' if they have not 'surrendered or lost [their] rights' through warring themselves,[33] is a better one not only than Trotsky's 'ties of class and family solidarity'; but also than this, sequel to the passage quoted earlier, from Kate Soper: 'if one is a socialist in outlook then one feels obliged to recognize that individuals not only have immediate personal rights and duties but are also answerable for the larger social consequences of their collective individual acts, and that consistent failure to act on the obligations incurred at the social level is legitimate ground for challenging their entitlement to respect for their personal rights.'[34] This is far too open-ended in range of possible application. It is unthinkable that it was so intended, but it would legitimate the most widespread violation of personal rights, which means violation of individuals and of lives. How many people are *not* guilty of failing in their social 'obligations', in Soper's sense, in a world that is rife with avoidable miseries, inequities and iniquities? It cannot be right virtually to erase the distinction, as this argument by implication does, between those actively warring to sustain oppression, and others less directly related to it: supporters and beneficiaries, passive accomplices or mere bystanders; people who, whatever their moral faults, guilts or evasions, have not – or at least have not yet – made themselves into a coercive barrier against realizing the legitimate rights of others. Unless, once more, it is allowed that the ethics of revolution may be about the punishment of sin, rather than about the removal of armed obstacles to liberation or justice. I assume they may not.

These individual rights constitute a limit upon consequentialist calculation. They cannot be disregarded in favour of, traded off against a hypothesis or speculation of there being, some greater benefit derivable from such trade – even if this supposed benefit is itself computed in terms of rights. That exercise might be legitimate, were the successful issue of revolutionary struggle millennial in character, a time and condition in which all would finally be well. We are surely over, if we ever really entertained, that kind of illusion. Whatever benefits real revolutions in a just cause may bring, each one is always a particular, a limited, even if it is a very large, step forward; and is a step always into new difficulties, new problems and conflicts, unforeseen and unforeseeable consequences; into uncertainties. That is if they win. Sometimes they lose, or lose for the time being. Against this background, these features of real as opposed to millenial revolutions, no one's life or person may be simply discounted for what are by their nature uncertain, sometimes highly speculative, projections – no one who has not taken the path of war by aggressing on behalf of tyranny or injustice; and in that case even they retain their rights against inhumane cruelty.

The question will be raised at this juncture whether individual rights against being killed or violated are then, in every other circumstance, absolute. They are all but absolute. If this answer is deemed to be insufficiently precise, its superiority over the meaningful alternatives to it appears to me compelling.[35] One such alternative is to say that the rights are indeed absolute, inviolable everywhere save when forfeited by their holders in the manner described. The trouble with this is that it is always possible to envisage cases (one has to kill an innocent person to avert a massacre of hundreds; or to save the population of a city; etc.) for which it would be conceded by all but a few doctrinaire fanatics that the moral horror of the consequences has – tragically – to be allowed to override the rights of the innocent. Examples like that are much rarer in reality than they are in philosophical discussion but cannot be excluded unfortunately from the situations of extremity which compose wars and revolutions. On the other hand, we make the force of these rights too weak if we say (something like): they must be respected by and large, or must be respected except when there are important or urgent competing considerations. That would render them, for present purposes, nugatory. For, the situations we are talking about just are, *ex hypothesi*, ones full of urgency, full of competing considerations of the gravest kind. In order, therefore, to have the necessary force to constrain and limit what is done in a just revolutionary cause, the rights must be treated as all but absolute.

That is to say that they may be overridden if and only if doing so is the sole means of averting imminent and certain disaster. I repeat: the sole means; and disaster which is otherwise imminent and certain. This is a proviso of impending moral catastrophe. What it permits is to do a moral wrong in order to escape some very terrible consequence. But it is, then, precisely a wrong that is done. Justifiable in one perspective, it remains unjustifiable in another. 'It does not become *all right*.'[36] It is produced out of an irresoluble conflict between two types of moral reasoning, the reckoning of consequences and respect for individual rights. Someone's rights *have* to be overridden; but *overridden* is what they have to be. It is a tragedy, an unavoidable crime. All the more reason so to specify the circumstances of exception as maximally to ensure that people's rights against violence may not be disregarded lightly. And if it is said that even the stipulation of impending catastrophe cannot eliminate difficult borderline cases and, therewith, the possible commission of avoidable under the heading of unavoidable crimes, that cannot be denied. All the same, it does put much, and quite clearly so, beyond acceptable limits: the acceptable limits of a just revolutionary struggle.

In his argument that revolution, as tendentially a form of war, cannot be limited by 'abstract norms', Trotsky derides 'the bourgeois pacifist who wants to "humanize" warfare by prohibiting the use of poison gases, the bombardment of unfortified cities, etc.' The argument backfires. It acquits those engaged in warfare of any responsibility for what they do by blaming the phenomenon – war – itself. It is a variant of the 'war is hell' theme and, as such, anticipates arguments of the same general form which were to be used, a few years later, by Harry Truman and his advisers to justify the atomic bombing of Hiroshima and Nagasaki.[37] It is too easy. That a revolution is likely to involve violence; that the opponents of freedom and equality, democracy or socialism, are generally ready to use massive, horrifying violence; that the struggle against them is then a war, and as a war, a realm of the most brutal necessity; none of this can legitimate a way of thinking, or at least of speaking, which would relax all moral limits by making the activity of war itself the culprit for anything that the participants in it might do. If there are indeed circumstances to make some moral crimes unavoidable, it is still necessary to have the rules and restraints which define them as crimes and which serve as a barrier against the avoidable ones. Socialists surely have good reason to be on their guard against forms of argument that are used to throw off all ethical constraints from around the conduct of war; and that were used, specifically, to justify opening the latest and potentially the most lethal chapter in the history of human warfare.

III

Where there are established parliamentary democracies, with a set of basic civil and political rights and freedoms protected under law, there is no right of revolution on account of tyranny. There is a right of social revolution − on account of grave injustice − against the capitalist forms of power, wealth and privilege over which these democracies preside, but the thing is complicated by the claim the latter make to democratic legitimacy. For, the claim rests upon a presumption, explicit or implicit, of popular consent, and the presence of consent − even be it granted that it is less than full-blooded or universal, that it is qualified in all sorts of ways, shades into mere acquiescence or apathy, and so on − must partially weaken the force of any judgement of grave injustice.

I carry water every day a long distance to your house and at some cost in time and energy to myself. You say, 'Thank you very much.' I do it under threat of violence and would not other-wise. The relation is exploitative. Now, on the other hand, I carry the water every day, even though it takes time and is hard, because you are a weak and aged friend and cannot do it. I do it willingly, as a favour. There is no injustice in the relation. These are delibera-tely simple, extreme, examples. It is possible to construct a range of intermediate ones in which the ingredients of force and consent are more mixed and are thrown together with others still: habit and custom, ideology or illusion, etc. But further examples are unnecessary to my point: that the stronger the basis for a presump-tion of freely given consent to some particular set of social relations, the more qualified must be the practical conclusions that can be drawn from any judgement of injustice pertaining to them. In the present case, no revolutionary attempt, especially as involving violence, is justifiable in the light only of a philosopher's − or revolutionary's, or political group's − judgement that the social order is unjust. That judgement needs to be 'proven', in a manner of speaking, by a recognition, on the part of those on the receiving end of the unjust relations, that such is indeed their character.

This amounts to saying, first, that any project of social revolution has to demonstrate its democratic credentials; and second, that if it is to contest the democratic legitimacy of those limited types of democracy that exist in some capitalist societies, it will have to offer, and then win democratic support for, an alternative form of democratic legitimacy. The road of social revolution cannot therefore simply bypass the institutions of parliamentary democracy. It either runs through them as a gateway or, being blocked in the attempt, shows in practice that they are not one, but are a fortress rather, a bastion against social revolution, just or democratic as may be; and shows the location of a genuine gateway at the same time.

We come here upon old and well-known arguments. This road, in theory and dispute, is a much beaten track. I tread it myself again now briefly, in order only to make one observation pertinent to the ethics of revolution. I am concerned, then, with two broad types of strategic viewpoint, which may be called, for short, the 'gateway' and the 'bastion' hypotheses. (I reject a more familiar terminology of 'parliamentary' versus 'extra-parliamentary' roads to socialism, for reasons to be set forth in a moment.) In either case, though, it should be emphasized, it is the ethics of socialist *revolution* that are under discussion: I set aside the viewpoint sometimes known as gradualism. According to this, there is no need for revolution at all because socialism can be achieved bit by bit over a very long period. At the end of the line, there will have been a radical transformation but there will have been no revolution in the sense that matters here, because of the long drawn out, the piecemeal, albeit cumulatively fundamental, nature of the process.[38] I set this conception aside as irrelevant to the ethical issues involved, irrespective of whether or not it offers a feasible path to socialism; that is, even if (as I doubt) it does. For, 'can' does not imply 'ought'. If capitalist societies are gravely – integrally – unjust and a democratic basis can be won for their more or less rapid transformation, it is not then clear what moral consideration would speak in favour of preferring a process which might take two or three hundred or more years.

I now set aside, also, extreme variants of the 'gateway' and 'bastion' hypotheses. It does not matter whether or not anyone really subscribes to these in such an exaggerated form, though the opponents of each can be found who will so present or caricature the view they reject. The two extremes are, in any case, limit positions to be set aside in trying to delineate the strategic terrain in a more realistic way. Let us call them, respectively, 'pure' parliamentarism and 'pure' insurrectionism. According to the first, socialist transformation can be achieved by a political process in all essentials identical to the normal passage of parliamentary legislation. A socialist party is elected on the basis of its revolutionary programme and this is carried through into law and public policy. Its implementation is the socialist revolution. The state that sees it through remains intact. According to the second conception, by contrast, the battle for socialism takes place outside the (bourgeois) parliamentary arena and against the existing state. It is a mass, extra-parliamentary struggle, throwing up alternative democratic institutions and, with them, a situation of dual power. The victory of this new democracy over the old state, which is destroyed, is the indispensable condition of social revolution.

Now, given both the enormity of the tasks entailed in any socialist transformation of society and the extent of probable opposition to it, it is unthinkable that the project could be accomplished on pure parliamentarist lines. It would require as a complement the most intensive commitment and participation, active struggle, by very large numbers of people outside parliament; and in a sufficiently structured and organized way that there is good reason to stress the vital role of an extra-parliamentary democracy alongside the parliamentary one. However composed, moreover – of workers', consumers' and neighbourhood committees, local or regional councils, campaign bodies, minority movements, or whatever – if it is indeed socialism that is brought into being, then much of this other, participatory democracy, of the structures and the spirit of it, would have to survive the work of revolution itself, as the material of a more democratic political order. To

put the same thing otherwise, even if there is some historical continuity between the parliamentary democracy at the origin of this
whole process and the polity that emerges from it, this could not
be exactly the same state, unchanged in its fundamental features.
If not, as in the Leninist canon, 'smashed', it would have been
significantly transformed.

On the other hand, the pure insurrectionist approach will be
embarrassed to explain how a socialist party, or coalition of parties,
or movement, which had been capable of guiding a struggle for
socialism to the point of dual power, had been able to win a
democratic mandate for its revolutionary project within institutions
of workers' or popular or participatory democracy lying across
the territory of an entire country – how such a political formation
could be incapable of winning significant representation within
an existing democratic parliament. If it can begin to found a new
democratic legitimacy, it must have some possibility of creating
a space, a platform, a point of struggle for it within the old. Simply
bypassing the democratic institutions that exist is not, therefore,
a serious hypothesis. In addition, the insistence, under the rubric
of 'smashing' the state, on a total discontinuity between bourgeois-
democratic and projected socialist polities has tended to obscure
for too many revolutionary socialists the value of certain norms
and institutions which any real socialist democracy would need
to incorporate: amongst them, a national representative assembly
elected by direct universal suffrage, some separation of powers,
the independence of judicial from political processes, the protection of basic individual rights, a constitutionally guaranteed political pluralism. Even if a socialist democracy can only emerge by
replacing the institutions of the old state, there is reason to dwell
on a line of continuity here all the same.

Thus qualified, the 'gateway' and the 'bastion' hypotheses
remain different. Each now comprehends, as is necessary in the
given context for any minimally serious strategic approach, both
a parliamentary and an extra-parliamentary dimension to socialist
revolution, both a continuity and a discontinuity of political forms.
But they still differ, and critically, in this: the former hypothesis

forbids, what the latter one countenances, a point of constitutional rupture. For, in the 'gateway' view socialist transformation must, while in the 'bastion' view it need not, derive its legitimacy from the parliamentary source.

I defend the ethical basis of the 'bastion' view. The other one says more, probably, or at least implies more, than it knows. By treating the prevailing, parliamentary legitimacy as the single acceptable origin of any projected socialist legitimacy it places allegiance to an existing state above considerations of democracy or justice. To see the point, one only has to allow here what has been much emphasized in the earlier part of this essay: the inherently, the deeply, uncertain character of all revolutionary situations. So, try to envisage the broad lines of such a situation with both its parliamentary and extra-parliamentary facets. These two democracies, let us concede, under some conditions could cohere into a more or less well-articulated assault on the positions of capitalist power and wealth; into a successful assault. But how, other than dogmatically, could it be ruled out in advance that they might not so cohere? That, for example, a particular parliamentary assembly might try to use what was left of its present term – which could be some *years* – to resist very urgent demands coming with clear, formally expressed and overwhelming support from the extra-parliamentary democratic institutions? Or that other forces, including other forces within the state, might move, and some of them violently, to block the parliamentary gateway? One only has to allow the possibility. Must the justification, the legitimacy, of socialist revolution in the parliamentary-democratic capitalist countries, come from one specific kind of institutional link with the past? It will come, if it does come, from securing a democratic foundation for putting an end to social relations that are unjust.[39]

Notes

1. It follows Anthony Arblaster, 'What Is Violence?', in Ralph Miliband and John Saville, eds., *The Socialist Register 1975*, London 1975, pp. 227–39.

2. Michael Walzer, 'The Moral Standing of States', *Philosophy and Public Affairs* 9, 1979–80, p. 215.

3. John Locke, *The Second Treatise of Civil Government*, Chapter XIX, paragraph 228. And see paragraphs 149, 199, 201, 212, 229.

4. See Barrington Moore Jr, *Reflections on the Causes of Human Misery*, London 1972, pp. 25–8.

5. As this contrast may also be expressed, 'Are capitalist states capitalist because there has been no socialist revolution, or has there been no socialist revolution because they are capitalist?' I owe the formulation to Göran Therborn who used (something like) it at a colloquium some years ago.

6. Ted Honderich, *Violence For Equality*, Harmondsworth 1980, p. 35. (Emphasis in the original – as generally here unless stated otherwise.) The sentiment vaguely echoes that of Mark Twain I have used as epigraph. Honderich has some compelling ways of focusing one's mind on the 'other' compelling order of fact. See, for example, pp. 16–20, 26; and p. 141, lines 16–21. On the definitional point, see again Arblaster, 'What Is Violence?', pp. 239–43.

7. I discuss and criticize the notion of prefiguration at length in *The Legacy of Rosa Luxemburg*, Verso, London 1976, pp. 133–73.

8. See, respectively, Kai Nielsen, 'On Justifying Revolution', *Philosophy and Phenomenological Research* 37, 1976–7, pp. 527–8, and Barrington Moore Jr, *Political Power and Social Theory*, New York 1962, p. 206. See also the same author's *Reflections on the Causes of Human Misery*, pp. 25–30; Mihailo Markovic, 'Violence and Human Self-Realisation', in his *The Contemporary Marx*, Nottingham 1974, p. 169; and David Miller, 'The Use and Abuse of Political Violence', *Political Studies* 32, 1984, p. 417.

9. This might well be the sense of Herbert Marcuse, 'Ethics and Revolution', in Richard T. De George, *Ethics and Society*, London 1968, pp. 139–40, 142–6; and is the sense of Honderich's argument in *Violence For Equality*, pp. 45–51, 163–5, 182–7; albeit that Honderich, for his part, is explicit in rejecting the terminology of 'calculation' or 'computation' for one of 'comparison'.

10. The view is put forward apropos war by David Luban, 'Just War and Human Rights', *Philosophy and Public Affairs* 9, 1979–80, pp. 174–6.

11. Leon Trotsky et al., *Their Morals and Ours*, New York 1966, p. 41. And cf. Marcuse, 'Ethics and Revolution', p. 146.

12. 'The Moralists and Sycophants against Marxism', in Trotsky, *Their Morals and Ours*, p. 48 – and see his earlier *Terrorism and Communism*, Ann Arbor 1961, pp. 22, 58, for similar arguments: 'Who aims at the end cannot reject the means.... If the socialist revolution requires a dictatorship ... it follows that the dictatorship must be guaranteed at all cost'; '...the revolution does require of the revolutionary class that it should attain its end by all methods at its disposal.'

13. *Their Morals and Ours*, pp. 19–20, 46–7, 53; and Lenin, 'The Proletarian Revolution and the Renegade Kautsky', *Collected Works*, Moscow 1960–70, Volume 28, p. 236. Cf. Barrington Moore, *Reflections*, p. 39.

14. Arblaster tentatively offers both possibilities; in Marcuse the point is unclear. These arguments are from: Marcuse, 'Ethics and Revolution', pp. 140–

41, and two essays by Anthony Arblaster, 'Bread First, Then Morals' and 'Means and Ends in the Struggle for Socialism'. The first of the two is in David McLellan, ed., *Socialism and Morality*, London 1990; it is the second (unpublished) essay that has the specific exclusions. Cf. also on this matter Kai Nielsen, 'On the Ethics of Revolution', *Radical Philosophy* 6, Winter 1973, p. 19.

15. See Locke, *The Second Treatise of Civil Government*, Chapter XIX, paragraphs 223, 225, 230.

16. Steven Lukes, *Marxism and Morality*, Oxford 1985, pp. xiii, 141–2, 146–8; and see Arblaster, 'Bread First, Then Morals'; and Kate Soper, 'Marxism and Morality', *New Left Review* 163, May/June 1987, pp. 111–13.

17. Michael Walzer, *Just and Unjust Wars*, New York 1977, p. 227.

18. Soper, 'Marxism and Morality', pp. 112–13.

19. The description is from Phillip Van Niekerk, 'Ends and Nasty Means', *New Statesman*, 8 November 1985, p. 19. In general, my information is from newspaper coverage of the period. I have confined myself to using only what was widely reported.

20. See Walzer, *Just and Unjust Wars* (cited hereafter as Walzer), p. 21. The extent of my debt to Walzer's book will be plain to anyone familiar with it, as it will from the frequent reference here made to it. I should like, all the same, to acknowledge the debt more formally.

21. Walzer, pp. 41–3; and cf. Thomas Nagel, 'War and Massacre', *Philosophy and Public Affairs* 1, 1971–72, pp. 133–4.

22. Walzer, pp. 137, 144–6; Nagel, 'War and Massacre', pp. 139–40. For argument about the notion of 'innocence', see further George I. Mavrodes, 'Conventions and the Morality of War', *Philosophy and Public Affairs* 4, 1974–75, pp. 117–31, and Robert K. Fullinwider, 'War and Innocence', *Philosophy and Public Affairs* 5, 1975–76, pp. 90–97.

23. See Walzer, pp. 199–204.

24. Amilcar Cabral, *Revolution in Guinea*, London 1969, pp. 103–5; and Basil Davidson, *The Liberation of Guiné*, Harmondsworth 1969, pp. 96, 146–7. PAIGC: the African Independence Party of Guiné and the Cape Verde Islands. ANC: the African National Congress. For statements of the latter, see, for instance, the interview with Oliver Tambo in *The Guardian*, 5 November 1985, and the speech of his reported in the same paper, 10 January 1986. The second of these, it has to be said, is less unambiguous than the first.

25. Walzer, p. 198.

26. *Their Morals and Ours*, pp. 31–2, 46–7.

27. Walzer, pp. 151–9.

28. As well as his book, there is also a shorter piece by Michael Walzer addressed to it: see 'Political Action: The Problem of Dirty Hands', *Philosophy and Public Affairs* 2, 1972–73, pp. 160–80.

29. Nagel, 'War and Massacre', pp. 140–41.

30. See reports by David Beresford in *The Guardian*, 15 February and 29 May 1986.

31. From, respectively, David Beresford, 'The Killing of Maki Shosana', *The*

Guardian, 26 July 1985, and Allister Sparks, 'The Road to Revolution', *The Observer*, 28 July 1985.

32. Victor Serge, *Memoirs of a Revolutionary 1901–1941*, London 1963, p. 282. The passage is also cited in Lukes, *Marxism and Morality*, p. 122.

33. Walzer, p. 135.

34. Soper, 'Marxism and Morality', p. 113.

35. I here follow, yet once more, Michael Walzer; for this and the next paragraph, see Walzer, pp. 228–32, 251–5, and *passim*; and also his 'Political Action: The Problem of Dirty Hands', pp. 171, 174.

36. Nagel, 'War and Massacre', p. 136–7; and cf. pp. 126, 142–3.

37. Trotsky, *Their Morals and Ours*, p. 47. Walzer, p. 265; and see also pp. 32–3.

38. See my definition of revolution at the beginning of this essay.

39. In thinking about the issues that occupy the major part of this essay I was helped by some discussions I had with friends. I thank them all, Paul Cammack, Mary Simons, Hillel Steiner, Ralph and Angela Young; as well as my closest friend, Adèle. Given the subject matter, I am more than just conventionally obliged to add here that none of the above necessarily agrees with the views I have expressed.

PART TWO

The Ways of
'Discourse'

3

Post-Marxism?

Times change and people change. Their ideas change; develop, progress – and regress. There can be gradual change within a more or less stable intellectual framework. And there can also be sharper breaks, mutations of outlook in which one thing is renounced and another embraced. But each person has to take his leave or make her peace, as the case may be, in a way conformable to his or her own sense of dignity.

We may cite the example of Eduard Bernstein, in the history of Marxist thought the first and the best-known so-called revisionist. Anyone at all familiar with his work will know that what he achieved – or perpetrated – was not truly a revision; it was a renunciation. The judgement is based not on any narrow or sectarian definition of what Marxism is but on the broadest, most inclusive definition possible. Bernstein challenged or set aside virtually every significant principle of Marxist thought. But he presented this as just a revision and it is not difficult to see why. For his political context and his audience were those of the German SPD, an avowedly Marxist party, with a Marxist programme, lineage and traditions, and within which Bernstein himself was an old and respected figure. Not only his public but also his own past will have weighed upon him, long-standing member of the organization, party editor, the friend and literary executor of Friedrich Engels. In the circumstances, it is understandable that he should have claimed only to be updating Marx's ideas in the light of contemporary developments, and not, as he really was, to be rejecting them lock, stock and barrel.

A first caution is needed here. No suggestion is intended that a person's relation to his or her own ideas is a purely, or even primarily, instrumental one, consciously calculated for advantage. In general, at any rate, one is bound to assume sincerity. Other things can be at work, all the same, than just the internal exigencies of an intellectual process.

Yesterday and Today

These remarks bear directly upon today. In the advanced capitalist world from the mid-1960s a generation of intellectuals was radicalized and won for Marxism. Many of them were disappointed in the hopes they formed – some of these wild but let that pass – and for a good while now we have been witnessing a procession of erstwhile Marxists, a sizeable portion of the generational current they shared in creating, in the business of finding their way 'out' and away. This exit is always presented, naturally, in the guise of an intellectual advance. Those of us unpersuaded of it cannot but remind its proponents of what they once knew but seem instantly to forget as they make their exit, namely, that the evolution of ideas has a social and material context. We cannot help wondering how far their recent trajectory may have been influenced by a range of factors which they themselves would doubtless prefer to overlook: the pressures upon them of age and professional status; the pressures of the political time and environment we have been passing through, not very congenial, in the West at least, to the sustenance of revolutionary ideas; and then the lure of intellectual fashion, a consideration not to be underrated by any means.

The life of the intellectual of the left is pulled by different forces.

There is, on the one hand, a moral commitment of some sort, however formulated; to socialism, the end of exploitation, human liberation, a decent existence at last for everyone. But there is also, on the other hand, a certain self-image, *as* intellectual, and amongst its constituents, the desire for recognition, and so, perhaps, originality, and the hope or the sense of being in the very van, not just abreast of the latest theoretical development but one of its actual partisans and sponsors. The force of the former, the gravitational pull of moral commitment, is a variable one, as this same intellectual is well enough aware while she or he understands Marx. It is stronger when materially manifested, so to speak, visibly represented in and supported by a social move-ment – that of the exploited and the otherwise oppressed – particu-larly on the march, in active struggle. It is much weaker where this is absent; or in defeat or retreat. The bare commitment, and the ultimate historical objectives, can come here to seem rather abstract and remote, so distant from a particular personal destiny as to be hardly related to it at all. In the light of what is intellectually on offer at this moment, the theoretical perspective which has most securely embodied the commitment and the objectives for more than a century – Marxism – may then begin to appear as old hat.

A second caution is now necessary. This is not the thesis of the inevitability of a growing political moderation and conserva-tism with age. There can be few socialists who were not once, at a point in youth or early adulthood, confronted by the patroniz-ing wisdom of maturity and told in effect that their socialism was wholly appropriate to their years but otherwise misguided, as they would themselves eventually come to realize. At the time, all of us will have felt such counsel to be false and some of us now know that it was so. There is no inevitability about it. We are still socialists and have been able to learn too from those who sustained the idea to the very end. A couple of decades on, how-ever, it is impossible not to acknowledge a certain truth in that cynical counsel, even if another than the one that was intended. For, casualties and departures there are. Once beyond the enthusiasm of their early years, with its follies, to be sure, but with a capacity also for energetic and disinterested solidarity, some *will* be carried away, more attentive now to other voices: so-called realism, resignation, or merely candid self-interest.

A couple of decades on, from the late 1960s. To be a Marxist then was, in a manner of speaking, the thing, or if not *the* thing, certainly something. But it did carry a commitment and this has become more difficult with the times. In such a situation, straight-forward renegacy – if I may risk this expression – is always possible, of course. One can reject Marxism for some old and standard alternative: Christianity, liberalism or what have you. But there are reasons why a more disguised route may well be taken. One of them is self-protection against the idea of a volte-face, since people do not generally like to admit having turned around. Another is the bond a person already has with a given audience or milieu and the reluctance to sever it completely; or, put rather more concretely, an awareness of the great intellectual and moral authority Marxism continues to enjoy, notwithstanding its many enemies and critics. And a third is the consideration, already mentioned, of wishing to be an up-to-the-minute thinker. These reasons have nothing to do with a will to deceive. They concern the sources of respect and of self-respect; that which one has and that which one wants. Again, everyone must settle accounts in a way compatible with their own pride and dignity.

Beyond Marxism

With these observations as a backdrop I want to discuss Ernesto Laclau and Chantal Mouffe's *Hegemony and Socialist Strategy: Towards a Radical Democratic Politics* – which styles itself 'post-Marxist'.[1] This is not because I consider the book to be theoretically worthwhile in any substantive respect. I do not. Indeed, it is a product of the very advanced stage of an intellectual malady, in a sense I shall presently explain; and it is theoretically profligate, dissolute, in ways I shall also seek to demonstrate, more or less any ideational combination or disjunction being permitted here, without regard for normal considerations of logic, of evidence or of due proportion. But the book is interesting nevertheless for at least two reasons. The first is that, as Ellen Meiksins Wood has said, it is 'beautifully paradigmatic': it brings together virtually all the key positions of a sector of the European left moving rightwards;[2] and the second is the post-Marxist claim itself.

This has, let it be noted, relative, at least, to the likes of Bernstein's 'revision' of Marxism, a certain plain-speaking accuracy. The authors announce a clear break. They are now beyond Marxism. There is a bit more to be said about it, however. For, they do also insist on reminding us that Marxism is where they have come from. Whilst allowing that their present conclusions could have been arrived at by other paths and ones 'alien to the socialist tradition' – to which one can only say: verily! – they are mindful of their own past and have chosen, therefore, to proceed from 'certain intuitions and discursive forms' within it.[3] Could they be mindful too in this of links they are for the time being content to preserve? I shall suggest, in any event, that the tendency in recent Marxism most germane to the construction of their current outlook is merely the bad side of something which was two-sided in the hands of its originator. And then there is the exact meaning in which they may be said now to be 'beyond' Marxism. At the point in time, thought and politics they have so far reached, the post-Marxist tag no doubt has a nicer ring to Laclau and Mouffe's ears than would the alternative, 'ex-Marxist'. It evokes an idea of forward movement rather than a change of colours, what purports to be an advance or progress, and all decked out in the finery of discourse theory. My contention will be that at the heart of this post-Marxism there is an intellectual vacuum, a term I use advisedly: both a theoretical and a normative void, with some very *old* viewpoints, prejudices and caricatures around it.

I mount, then, what is in a certain sense a defence of Marxism; in a certain sense only, because it is to be doubted that anyone not already a Marxist will be persuaded to become one just by virtue of what I have to say here. But my purpose is more limited.

It is to show that if there are good reasons for not being, or for ceasing to be, a Marxist, so-called post-Marxism isn't one of them.

I

Let us try to orient ourselves. These are some standard Marxist positions rejected in Laclau and Mouffe's book. In the first place: that objective, or structural, class position is the primary historical determinant of social and political identities and alignments; that the relations of production (or economic structure) enjoy(s) explanatory primacy; that politics and ideology are, correspondingly, secondary; that the metaphor of base and superstructure is a theoretically viable one.[4] Then: that the working class has an objective interest in socialism; that it is valid to speak of the *objective* interests of a class; that there are structural tendencies towards unification of the working class, for all the factors which fragment and divide it; and that as compared with other potentially radical social forces, it has a special – what these writers, in a noteworthy usage, like to call a 'privileged' – connection with the struggle for socialism.[5] Denied also: that socialism itself, the abolition of capitalist production relations, is the crucial strategic goal within the project of emancipatory social transformation (rather than, as Laclau and Mouffe now see it, just a dimension of 'radical democracy', or of 'the democratic revolution') and defines the fundamental moment, the decisive point of revolutionary rupture, in this epochal process of transformation.[6] And even, finally: that society and history can be rendered intelligible by some unifying principle or principles, or within a unified framework, of explanation and knowledge (something rejected however, it must be emphasized in this case, only incompletely and without the trouble of intellectual consistency, since with this as with every other assertion of relativism, its advocates necessarily contradict themselves so soon as they venture explanatory categories of their own).

Now, I think it fair to say that there is nothing in this catalogue of denials that could really surprise anyone. They are all thoroughly familiar. With the possible exception only of the last of them, they will be readily assented to by ordinary, old-fashioned *non*-Marxists. To discover what could be *post*-Marxist here, we must proceed a bit, therefore.

Expressive Totality

We will find, at least, something taken from one school of Marxism and taken further, so to say. Across its several particular propositions and negations, Laclau and Mouffe's argument is organized around a single all-embracing constructional principle. This is the division between the *simple* and the *complex*, or the *closed* and the *open*. On one side, there is simplicity, a desire for theoretical closure; on the other side, the recognition of complexity and openness. That is how the intellectual universe is divided.

In attempting to understand social and historical processes, there are those – the Marxist tradition in its entirety, but other thinkers as well – who reduce the complexity, diversity, multiformity, disparateness, plurality and opacity of it all to the simple, the single, the unified, the transparent. Thereby they theorize a closure. Determined from, and intelligible by reference to, one foundation or origin, society becomes a closed totality, is conceived, in the word of a less familiar idiom, as *sutured*. Because of this, of 'the conviction that the social is sutured at some point, from which it is possible to fix the meaning of any event',[7] Marxism is deficient. *Hegemony and Socialist Strategy* is replete with the language of its deficiency: 'reductionist problematic' for obvious reasons, 'monist' and 'profoundly monist', because of the idea of the unique foundation, 'essentialist discourse' (... 'essentialist core', 'essentialist vision', 'essentialist conception', 'orthodox essentialism' ...), because this foundation is an essence of the social, and 'economist paradigm', because it is the economy; 'classism', because of the primary role accorded to its constituent classes; 'stagist paradigm', because of the necessary stages through which it evolves,

67

'rationalism' and 'rationalist paradigm', because of the belief in the transparent intelligibility of the social whole; and still more, on account of the closed or fixed or *a priori* conceptual basis. And then a variety of combinations: like 'essentialist monism', and 'classist economism', and 'economist stagism'; 'essentialist apriorism' also; 'essentialist fixity'; 'the internal rationality and intelligibility of a closed paradigm', 'a purely classist and closed view of the world', 'the sutured space of a rationalist paradigm', and so on.[8]

But there are those, on the other hand, Laclau and Mouffe themselves particularly, who insist on facing up to social complexity, diversity and the rest and, to this end, on 'the open, non-sutured character of the social',[9] which has no essence except negatively speaking: 'we must begin by renouncing the conception of "society" as founding totality of its partial processes. We must, therefore, consider the openness of the social as the constitutive ground or "negative essence" of the existing.'[10] In other terms: 'the mere idea of a centre of the social has no meaning at all.'[11] Unification and closure are, here, accordingly impossible: 'The moment of the "final" suture never arrives.'[12]

Nourished though it plainly has been from other sources as well, readers of Althusser's writings will easily recognize within this polar contrast an old friend and familiar foe, by name, the 'spiritual' or 'expressive' totality. The concept was used by him in the effort to remove Marx's mature work out of the shadow of Hegel, in whose thought, Althusser argued, the apparent complexity of the social whole was *merely* apparent since its multiple aspects were always traceable and therefore reducible in the end to an original common essence, itself a moment or stage in the development of the world spirit. The diverse and manifold appearances of the Hegelian totality were expressions of this unique spiritual essence, which was present and more or less legible in them all. The outwardly complex thus gave way to the essentially simple.[13] Against every such simplifying tendency, Althusser himself emphasized the reality of 'overdetermination'; and Laclau and Mouffe in turn – as they put it, 'radicalizing' this last concept[14] – now propose openness and the like. But a crucial shift has taken place. The concepts in question were deployed by Althusser to inscribe a line within Marxism between what he saw as its authentic and its deviant forms. Laclau and Mouffe redraw the line between the whole of Marxism, this erstwhile mentor of theirs included, all vitiated beyond the hope of any remedy, and the theoretical outlook they have come now to favour.

The Continent of Theoretical Error

It would be wrong, however, to pick out only the discontinuity in this use they make of 'essentialism' and its cognates, for there is also a clear and unhappy continuity to be observed – beyond that involved in the bare employment of these categories, that is. The Althusserian spiritual or expressive totality had, to put it crudely, both a good and a bad side. The good, what was valuable in the context of much Marxological discussion of the time, was that it created an opening for Marx the materialist historian, student of economy and polity, social scientist, making this figure of him visible again to a new generation from behind the obscuring image of just one more philosopher, ethical, speculative or visionary. It warned against the temptation of preordained harmonies, any too facile story of the progress of the world, be it even one about human species-being, and laying stress upon the scientific ambition of Marx's enterprise, stressed with it the contradiction, the specificity of 'levels' and of detail, the complexity indeed, of the domain and the material that had to be theoretically assimilated and understood. To this extent, it could point Althusser's readers, notwithstanding some severe confusions of his own in the matter, towards the empirically based character and rational spirit of the enterprise: the labour and difficulty of it, the process of change inherent to it, the necessary movement of revision and correction. The bad side of the same concept, however, was the disposition it appeared to encourage in its author to bring the entire intellectual universe down to a sort of Manichean opposition. Outside the tightly drawn circle of Althusserian, overdetermined truth, the sin of expressive totality was *everywhere*, sometimes on the strength of a single concept or argument, sometimes on the strength of no more than the accusation itself. And it united the most seemingly diverse intellectual phenomena, rendering them unwittingly complicit with one another. Hegel and empiricism, economism and humanism, historicism and rationalism; Hegelian-izing Marxism and Marxism of the Second International; Marxism of the Second International again, humanism likewise and – Stalinism: all of these and more linked up in one gigantic equation of reductionist error. Save for a very few – Marx in maturity, Lenin, Mao, and these not exempt from it altogether – there was scarcely a thinker of Marxist pedigree on whom the taint of that error did not lie exceedingly heavy: from Engels and Luxemburg, through Korsch and Lukács, to Gramsci, Sartre, Della Volpe, and beyond.

Of course, and so as not to oversimplify for my own part, a certain diversity, also, was conceded here and sometimes, even, localized or mitigating merits would be signalled by Althusser and praised. But at bottom, beneath the whirl of difference, in the fundamental, underlying structures of thought, there always turned out to be, whether clearly expressed or lightly concealed, the same kind of deficiency: the reductionist assumption of an original essence. Indeed, the deep irony in this is that one of the best possible examples of an expressive totality is – so to put it – the Continent of Theoretical Error According to Althusser. It is a space in which a quite enormous variety of ideas, idioms, philosophical and cultural lineages, may be seen to derive from, for having been all but reduced to, a single common essence, that species of error which Laclau and Mouffe today freely call 'essentialism'. It is this less salutary side of Althusser's own use of the notion of expressive totality, his readiness to suspect and detect it on all sides, that I had in mind in speaking earlier of an intellectual malady. It was a mischievous part of his legacy, one very soon disencumbered by others of the seriousness and rational commitment of his overall purpose, for the generous dealing out of theoretical anathemas; against all other Marxisms or, if necessary, against Marxism itself.

The same thing, in any case, is now to be found in *Hegemony and Socialist Strategy* but it is much more advanced than with Althusser – in the way that a malady, and not that a theory, advances. There is the same Manichean division, albeit that Marxism as a whole has come to fall on the wrong side of it, and symptomatic of it the largesse with epithets of error, as also the sheer plurality of them. Monism or economism, classism or closure, transparency or sutured totality: so many names of theoretical failure, or so many names, rather, for variants of a single theoretical failure, since that is what it amounts to, 'essentialism'. And consequently we have here again the same irony as before, the category returning against its user: a whole continent of thought stalked by the one mistake, a veritable sutured totality of incorrect ideas. In one critical respect, however, things have gone much further. For, whilst the new truth which Laclau and Mouffe oppose to all this is generically similar to the Althusserian in favouring complexity, diversity and so forth, against simplicity and a belief in essences, the difference is that, now, virtually *any* framework of historical explanation, any principle of sociological *intelligibility*, can be condemned in the name of 'the openness and indeterminacy of the social'.[15] This is the meaning of such passages as that dismissing 'any a priori schema of unification', and as that referring to 'the rationalism of classical Marxism, which presented history and society as intelligible totalities constituted around conceptually explicable laws', and as that 'dissolving' the postulate of '"society" as an intelligible structure that could be intellectually mastered on the basis of certain class positions'.[16] Despite its abuses, Althusser's expressive totality was at least intended in an enlightening spirit: as a putative contribution to the project of scientific reason and research; in the old and worthy effort to understand and explain. Laclau and Mouffe have embraced an obscurantism, capable of disaparaging every explanatory project, because an 'essence' will always be discoverable in whatever principle or principles of explanation it may put forward. With him, Althusser, the bad was partially redeemed by the good. With them, it is redeemed by nothing and is just plain ugly. Later I shall come back to the irony I have identified here and show how it can be turned against our two authors to uncover the idleness of the game out of which they have fashioned a book.

All or Nothing At All

So that we may eventually reach this point, let us begin, however, with a simple question. How does it happen that, where for Althusser overdetermined complexity was the very heart of authentic Marxism, for Laclau and Mouffe something generically similar shows Marxism to be hopelessly vitiated? A preliminary answer is that Laclau and Mouffe just give a caricatured and impoverishing account of what Marxism is. To be absolutely precise about this: it is not that they deny all the strengths, insights, contributions of theoretical value, as they construe them, to be found in the work of Marxist *writers*. No, they too will notice and praise these, the compensating qualities in a fundamentally blemished oeuvre. But such elements of value are all stipulated as being *external* to the real parameters of Marxism, a positive contribution made in each case in spite and not because of the fact that the author was a Marxist, made against the genuine basis of his or her creed. In a nutshell, Marxism is defined by Laclau and Mouffe in the most uncompromisingly necessitarian or determinist, most rigidly economistic, and – if one must – most simplifyingly 'essentialist' terms; and then dismissed for being determinist, economist, 'essentialist'. I shall give two sorts of evidence for this claim: some examples of a recurring technique of argument; then, a summary of the treatment meted out here seriatim to a number of Marxism's more important thinkers. Just note first what is no doubt only a small corroborating sign, but such as is not to be overlooked in a text so emphatic about the importance of discourse and all its varieties. That is a certain patronizing way Laclau and Mouffe have with the use of capitals: writing, for instance, 'a whole conception of socialism which rests upon ... the role of Revolution, with a capital "r" ... and conceptually built around History in the singular'; and 'the essentialism of the traditional Left, which proceeded with absolute categories of the type "*the* Party", "*the* Class", or "*the* Revolution"'; and 'a discourse concerning the privileged points from which historical changes were set in motion – the Revolution, the General Strike.'[17] It is a parodying mode, this, reducing Marxism to a fragment of itself, and that the poorest, the whole tradition to a few dogmatic absolutes. Conceptual absolutism, we shall see forthwith, can also be in the eye – and mind – of the beholder.

A first example of it concerns recent Marxist discussion of the notion of relative autonomy, 'a dead end' according to the authors: 'In general, such attempts to explain the "relative autonomy of the State" were made in a framework that accepted the assumption of a sutured society – for example, through determination in the last instance by the economy – and so the problem of relative autonomy, be it of the State or of any other entity, became insoluble. *For, either the structural framework constituted by the basic determinations of society explains not only the limits of autonomy but also the nature of the autonomus entity – in which case that entity is another structural determination of the system and the concept of "autonomy" is redundant; or else the autonomous entity is not determined by the system, in which case it is necessary to explain where it is constituted, and the premise of a sutured society would also have to be discarded.* It is precisely the wish to combine this premise with a concept of autonomy inconsistent with it, that has marred most contemporary Marxist debate on the State.... If, however, we renounce the hypothesis of a final closure of the social, it is necessary to start from a plurality of political and social spaces which do not refer to any ultimate unitarian basis.'[18]

It is the point about the 'irreducible plurality of the social' again.[19] But observe the stark and unbending antithesis of the alternative we are presented with in support of it. *Either* the basic determinants explain the nature of as well as the limits on what is supposed to be relatively autonomous, so that it is not really autonomous at all; *or* it is, flatly, *not* determined by them and they cannot be basic determinants. These alleged determinants, in other words, either explain everything or determine nothing (the logic being quite general in scope: '... relative autonomy, be it of the State or of any other entity...'). They explain either all or nothing at all. This poses an uncomfortable choice for Marxists, naturally. Unable to say 'nothing' and remain what they are, they will have to say 'everything' and be criticized for reductionism. Or if, knowing they are not reductionists, they are unable to say 'everything', they must renounce the assumption of there being basic determinants ('the premise of a sutured society') and with it their Marxism. Put in still other terms, Laclau and Mouffe here deny to Marxism the option of a concept like relative autonomy. No wonder that it can only be for them the crudest sort of economism.

But why are we obliged by the inflexible alternative they define? We are not. It is the merest verbal edict, unsupported by even an attempt at persuasive advocacy. A length of chain secures me by the ankle to a stout post. This limits what I can do but also leaves me a certain freedom. I can stand or sit, read or sing. I cannot play a decent game of table tennis, however, and cannot attend social functions or political meetings at all. The chain not only limits me, negatively; it also compels me to certain actions. The way it is fixed to my leg, I must keep adjusting how it lies, otherwise it begins to hurt me. I must apply medicaments periodically to sores which develop around my ankle. And so on. Understanding my situation more or less, I say that I enjoy a relative autonomy: the chain and post are fundamental determinants of my lifestyle but they do still leave me scope for independent decisions. Now, what should I think of two passers-by, call them Chantal and Ernesto, who, hearing me so describe things, declare: 'This is a dead end – conceptually. For, either the chain and post explain both the nature and the limits of your autonomy and the concept of "autonomy" is redundant; or else your situation is not determined by them'? The reasoning is fatuous, it should be noted, irrespective of whether the chain is considered to be *the* fundamental, or merely *a* fundamental, determinant. It is the stronger of the claims that is relevant, *mutatis mutandis*, to what Marxists believe. But a tool need only be appropriate to the nature, and difficulty, of the task at hand. Against the austerity of Laclau and Mouffe's logic – a burden they impose on Marxism only, things becoming much more relaxed, as we shall see, on their own pre-ferred 'discursive' terrain – this example is enough to show that, between explaining everything and determining nothing, there are real determinants able merely to account for a great deal. No Marxist has to choose, consequently, between the most extrava-gant economic reductionism and what the authors here commend to us, just plurality. She or he can recognize, for example, that there are genuinely distinct types of polity within capitalist societies, important differences in the form of the capitalist state; within limits, always some variety of possible political outcomes; and still argue that capitalist relations of production, and the configuration of classes they define, are primary to the explanation of such poli-ties. Others, of course, can argue otherwise. Let them do so. This is no argument, just an absolutist stipulation.

Class Unity and Class Interests

Here is a second example. It arises this time from discussion of Rosa Luxemburg's *Mass Strike* pamphlet and the problem, which she addresses there, of the unification of the working class as a revolutionary force out of many heterogeneous elements. The heterogeneity, or fragmentation, is due to the existence of different categories of workers and of degrees of organization amongst them, the specificities of their prior experience or local traditions, the range of demands that motivate them and of struggles in which they are involved – to a diversity, then, of what are called 'subject positions' by Laclau and Mouffe. This is how the latter characterize the 'well-known alternative' Marxism confronts in the matter: 'either capitalism leads through its necessary laws to proletarianiza-tion and crisis; or else these necessary laws do not function as expected, in which case ... the fragmentation between different subject positions ceases to be an "artificial product" of the capitalist state and becomes a permanent reality.'[20] It is another stark anti-thesis. *Either* pure economic necessity bears the full weight of unifying the working class; *or* we simply have fragmentation. In the one case, obviously, there can be no significant place for a socialist *politics*; in the other, class subjects are not any longer central, and politics, whether socialist or not, is truly in command, since it is here that the entire business of forging unities has now to be conducted. But why may we not think that between this devil and that deep blue sea there is something else: notwithstanding the wide diversity, a common structural situation, of exploitation, and some common features, like lack of autonomy or interest at work, not to speak of sheer unpleasantness and drudgery, and some pervasive economic tendencies, proletarianizing ones amongst them, and such also as create widespread insecurity of employment; all of this providing a solid, objective *basis* – no more, but equally no less – for a unifying socialist politics? Why may we not? Only because the authors say so: 'either ... or', there is no other way. No wonder, again, that it is the most rigid economism that they present to us as Marxism.

The third example has to do with the ascription of objective interests. This last concept, according to Laclau and Mouffe, 'lacks any theoretical basis whatsoever', is 'little more than an arbitrary attribution ... by the analyst'. It only makes sense at all within an 'eschatological conception of history'. Once more referring, in this connection, to the heterogeneity of positions within the working class, they express the following opinion. 'Here, the alternative is clear: either one has a theory of history according to which this contradictory plurality will be eliminated *and an absolutely united working class will become transparent to itself at the moment of proletarian chiliasm* – in which case its "objective interests" can be determined from the very beginning; or else, one abandons that theory and, with it, any basis for privileging certain subject positions over others in the determination of the "objective" interests of the agent as a whole – in which case this latter notion becomes meaningless.'[21] The want of proportion in this is very striking.

Its excess, indeed, prompts the thought of a dim, half-conscious worry somewhere in the minds of those responsible for it, that what they can offer on behalf of their chosen side of the dichotomy is feeble and will be seen to be so unless the other side of it is made to look impossibly bad – a thought which, as it happens, exposes the whole style of argument under review. In any case, we must believe not only that the working class can become 'absolutely united', not only, even, that it will then be 'transparent to itself'; we must believe this, in addition, under the description, 'the moment of proletarian chiliasm'. On such conditions we may employ the concept of objective interests, and otherwise not. But, of course, what we may actually believe in is the possibility of relative, and not absolute, unity: that a *large majority* of the working class could become *sufficiently* united. We may think that it could become, not 'transparent to itself', but *more clear* about what is wrong with the bourgeois social order, and *persuaded* of there being a realistic alternative to it. We may consider that the revolutionary transformation of that social order, painfully difficult of achievement, would be, not a religious consummation or advent, just the condition for a marked *improvement* in millions of people's lives. And on the strength of *this* judgement – that it would be an improvement, for their health and their welfare, their possibilities of self-fulfilment and happiness, and one they could themselves come to recognize and fight for – we may hold that we are entitled to speak of objective interests.

So, the sole absolutes here lie in the absolutism of these imperious dichotomies. It is an argumentative procedure the reader may like to remember. '*Tertium non datur!*' But only for us: it will be observed later on, by contrast, what sort of latitude Laclau and Mouffe can willingly tolerate – for themselves.

An Irreducible Dualism

The same impoverishing view of Marxism as is contained in these exemplary antitheses emerges more systematically in the account we are given of the tradition, writer by writer. I shall briefly summarize the main lines of this account. Its secret, however, is disclosed at the very start, in the Introduction to *Hegemony and Socialist Strategy*. The concept of hegemony, it is announced there, denotes a relation incompatible with, rather than complementary to, the basic Marxist categories. This concept, which will be central to the theoretical construction the authors will for their part propose, which they want, in one movement, both to take and to free from the conceptual armoury of Marxism, introduces, so they argue, a social logic of contingency opposed to the necessitarian logic that is Marxism's own.[22] The theme begets another, unavoidably. If hegemony and notions similar to it are incompatible with Marxist categories, then the presence of such notions in the thought of any particular Marxist must be the sign of an incoherence. They may be there, but they are not there with full theoretical legitimacy. However they may testify to the knowledge, insight, perspicacity or innovativeness of the thinker in question, they can do no credit to Marxism itself. In fact, they testify to the crisis, not the creativity, of the paradigm. The name of this theme, of this incoherence and crisis, is *dualism*. Let us try to get the measure of it, beginning, where Laclau and Mouffe do, with Rosa Luxemburg.

In the great movement of mass actions which she summed up in the expression, 'the mass strike', Luxemburg saw the possibility of a revolutionary unification. Their rolling, more-or-less spontaneous course would tend to transcend the division between economic and political aspects of the struggle, to generalize partial into more far-reaching and comprehensive demands, to overcome the aforementioned fragmentation of the working class. The conception so far, according to the authors of *Hegemony and Socialist Strategy*, had much in its favour. Not only did it take as its point of departure the manifest realities of proletarian diversity and dispersion. It envisaged, also, a unifying process whose type is symbolic, because having to do with the flow and overflow of *meanings* as between one struggle and another. Said to be 'the highest point' of her analysis, this set Luxemburg's thought at a 'maximum distance' from Second International orthodoxy, far along the way towards recognizing the scope and nature of social contingency. But she could not go right through to the end. Had she done so, she would have had no reason to suppose the result of the unifying process to be a *class* unity. 'On the contrary, the very logic of spontaneism seems to imply that the resulting type of unitary subject should remain largely indeterminate.' Why could this subject not be a 'popular or democratic' one? What held her back, limiting 'the innovatory effects' of the logic of spontaneism, was her belief in objective laws of capitalist development. The two things, that logic and these laws, made up an 'irreducible dualism'. Here it is that we come upon the disjunction already discussed: either pure economic necessity or permanent fragmentation.[23]

The details will be different but the pattern always the same. From Kautsky to Gramsci, Max Adler to Louis Althusser, it will be dualism (and, of course, 'essentialism'), engulfing all of Marxist thought and not only that. Karl Kautsky, like Luxemburg well aware of the fragmentary tendencies and interests within the German working class, makes the party into a 'totalizing instance'. The vehicle of scientific Marxist theory, and vouchsafing thereby a mediating role to intellectuals, it constitutes 'an articulating nexus that cannot simply be referred to the chain of a monistically conceived necessity'; there is a space here for '*the autonomy of political initiative*'. However, this space, with Kautsky, is minimal; just the initial relation of exteriority between socialist theory and the working class. For, theory itself is the guarantor of an eventually unfolding necessity and conceives political identities, reductively, fixedly, as governed by the relations of production.[24] Antonio Labriola, on the other hand, proposes that the objective laws of history are morphological only, valid for the broad, underlying tendencies and no more; and so makes use of 'other explanatory categories' in order to grasp the complexity of social life. But as he cannot derive these, dialectically, from the morphological ones, since that would be 'to extend the effects of necessity' back out again to embrace the whole, such categories – mark this – are '*external to Marxist theory*'. His proposal too, then, 'could not but introduce a dualism'.[25] In turn, Austro–Marxism goes rather far in restricting the scope of historical necessity, expanding that of 'autonomous political intervention', bringing, indeed, 'a strictly discursive element into the constitution of social objectivity'. Adler on Kant, Bauer on nationality, Renner on law – all contribute. But they fail, again, 'to reach the point of breaking with dualism and eliminating the moment of "morphological" necessity.'[26]

Even those who reach the point, at least, of breaking with Marxism and are warmly commended for their astuteness in so doing, do not evade the long arm of this judgement. Though their treatment is not directly relevant to the account we are given of Marxism itself, it is relevant indirectly in showing just how difficult escape here can be. I will not, therefore, disrupt the sequence of this intellectual history by omitting them. Eduard Bernstein actually makes 'the break with the rigid base/superstructure distinction that had prevented any conception of the autonomy of the political'; achieves a 'rupture with orthodox determinism'. With him, 'the moment of political articulation' cannot, as it can with Kautsky, be reduced to movements of the infrastructure. Alas, this does not carry Bernstein far enough to avoid a form of dualism. He continues to allow, alongside the space of the free ethical subject, some residual space and truth to the causalities of orthodoxy. Worse still, he has replaced the 'essentialist connections' of orthodoxy with 'essentialist presuppositions' of his own: 'in this case, the postulate of progress as a unifying tendency'. The latter provides new '*totalizing contexts* which fix a priori the meaning of every event'.[27] Georges Sorel, by contrast, does *not* subscribe to an evolutionist belief in progress, recognizing possibilities of disintegration and decay. He sees Marxism, initially, as an ideological and moral force for the formation and orientation of a new social agent, the proletariat. Then, accepting the revisionist critique, he comes to substitute the notion of social *mélange* for that of objective totality and to conceive classes, not as structural locations, but as *blocs*, constituted through will, action, and open contestation with antagonists. This culminates in the idea of the general strike as a constitutive myth, with its components of sentiment, fiction and violence as solidarizing factors. In all, Sorel not only creates an area for contingency, as have the others, but tries also 'to think the specificity' of its logic. Has *he* made it, then? Has he escaped from the ubiquitous dualism? He has not. His 'politically or mythically reconstituted subject' is a class subject.[28]

Trotsky, Lenin, Gramsci

Returning to Marxism's own story, we arrive with Russian Social Democracy at hegemony proper, a venture, at first too hesitant, across class boundaries. Marxism's problem in Russia, the problem of the Russian revolution, was not any longer only that of the political formation of a proletarian unity out of pre-existing diversity. It was the devolution to the working class of tasks of the bourgeois revolution, owing to the weakness of the Russian bourgeoisie and in departure from the orthodox schema of stages. The theoretical result in the debates of the time was a novel relation (between proletarian agent and bourgeois tasks) called hegemony; 'a space of indeterminacy', expanding in scope from the Mensheviks through Lenin to a maximum in Trotsky. Having discovered and named this relation, however, the Russian Marxists contrived to make it 'invisible' again; reproducing within the theory of hegemony, it can by now be no surprise to learn, 'the spurious dualism' of the Second International. This was because the specifically Russian 'narrative' continued to be conceptually subordinate to the orthodox one – even in Trotsky, the theory of permanent revolution to the schema of stages – with the second providing a level and order of 'essences' that gave meaning to the first. What was connected in the hegemonic relation remained external to and unaffected by it: though devolving upon a proletarian agent, bourgeois tasks remained bourgeois; the identity of the agent, despite this new breadth of its tasks, was still seen as determined by its structural position, and class identity in general as 'constituted on the basis of the relations of production'.[29] The point, in fact, turns out to have compromised all of Leninism. To be sure, the

Leninist tradition did emphasize how the conditions of uneven development in the imperialist era made hegemonic relations indispensable to the revolutionary struggle by complicating the map of pure class antagonisms; and hence insisted on the function of leadership within a class *alliance*, a decisively political bond across structurally defined locations. But this relation was still conceived as an external one, leaving unaltered the class identities making up the alliance. Their interests were not formed, just *represented*, there. Instead of 'the efficacy of the political level in constructing social relations', consequently, politics was but 'a bare stage', the players upon it scripted from elsewhere.[30]

It was only Gramsci, according to Laclau and Mouffe, who 'radically subverted' the foundations of this long dualist epic, moving beyond the notion of an external alliance of classes. By a broadening of the perspective from the political to the intellectual and moral plane – the terrain of ideology – Gramsci could think in terms of the forging of a *historical bloc*, which was 'a higher synthesis, a "collective will"', with a set of shared ideas and values across different class positions. Here, the hegemonic link was not concealed but 'visible and theorized', the base/superstructure distinction transcended, and the guarantee of laws of history dispensed with. The social agents were no longer, strictly, classes, but such 'collective wills'. In Gramsci's analysis, we are told, 'the field of historical contingency has penetrated social relations more thoroughly than in any of the previous discourses: the social segments have lost those essential connections which turned them into moments of the stagist paradigm'; there is 'a new series of relations among groups which baffles (sic) their structural location within the ... schema of economism'. But then again, perhaps not. For, Gramsci's conception was 'ultimately incoherent', not yet quite beyond 'the dualism of classical Marxism', inwardly 'essentialist' after all. His problem? – 'the unicity of the unifying principle, and its necessary class character'. For him, that is to say, 'there must always be a *single* unifying principle in every hegemonic formation, and this (could) only be a fundamental class.' Determination by the economy had been reaffirmed.[31]

What, finally of Althusser? Althusser is hoist with his own petard. With the concept of overdetermination he is said to have reached out potentially towards the understanding of a specific and irreducible type of complexity, a *symbolic* one in fact, entailing 'a plurality of meanings'. It implied that society could have no essence, since there was no possibility of fixing upon its ultimate 'literality' or sense. But 'a growing closure led to the installation of a new variant of essentialism.' Determination in the last instance by the economy, actually incompatible with the concept of overdetermination, was the thesis responsible for this; 'exactly the same dualism' was its result.[32]

The Essence of the Story

Now, there is more than one way of looking at this tale of Marxism Laclau and Mouffe have told. The first is as a simple sort of intellectual game. I call it simple because the basic rules of it are clear and easy to grasp. You take some Marxist, any Marxist will do, and begin by showing how in deference to complicated historical realities he or she departed from a rigidly, an absolutely, determinist economism. This will not be difficult to show since even the most economistic of them has allowed some efficacy, however small, to political and/or other non-economic instances, but in any case the distance he or she has travelled that way will give a measure of his theoretical insight, her recognition of contingency or indeterminacy, their relative success in groping towards an adequate idea of hegemony, and so on. You then nail the thinker in question for 'essentialism'. To do that, you need only catch them out in the use of a central Marxist category. Which Marxist category it is precisely – objective laws of capitalism, class or class interest, the forces or the relations of production – and its exact role and weight in the writer's thought, are matters of indifference. It is its bare presence there that counts. At some point, finally, you should work in a reference to the resulting dualism. As we shall see, certain features of the game are not quite so straightforward, indeed rather strange. But this much anyone can learn to play. You may try it with some other Marxist writers – Herbert Marcuse, say, or Isaac Deutscher – analyses of whom in this mode we have thankfully been spared.

A second angle of vision follows directly from this first. As it is no trouble to catch a Marxist at the use of Marxist concepts, such being what composes his or her Marxism, the reproach of 'essentialism' levelled here at writers in the tradition is just the reproach that they remained Marxists, nothing more. To show, for example, that notwithstanding her ideas about spontaneity, Luxemburg, and despite emphasizing the importance of political alliances, Lenin, and even within his theory of hegemony, Gramsci, continued to deploy a structural concept of class, only tells those interested what they already know. It does not, as would be needed for the charge of 'essentialism' to have any bite, demonstrate that Luxemburg, Lenin or Gramsci took the concept as explaining and resolving everything; show a conceptual inflation of class on their part into the originative source of all social and historical processes. Integral to Laclau and Mouffe's own argument, on the contrary, is that in the generality of Marxist writing the basic structural categories of Marxism were *not* used as all-explanatory and sufficient. For their users, then, they were not everything. But they were something. And more than that, of course, they were something crucially important. To say 'essentialism' merely on this account, however, is to be willing to find the vice wherever there are organizing explanatory concepts, where there is any kind of categorial priority. It is a long, firm step into the darkness.

Is more confirmation of such nihilism wanted than is provided by the repeated triggering in the text, at every conceivable sort of encounter with a basic Marxist category, of one of the manifold terms pertaining to 'essence' and 'suture'? If so, it is surely given by the fate at Laclau and Mouffe's hands of their chosen non-Marxists. Bernstein went so far as to repudiate historical materialism in its fundamentals. Nevertheless, we are cautioned, he believed in progress and this tended to endow other beliefs of his with a certain overall meaning. Sorel, then: he renounced

both historical materialism and faith in progress. He clung, however, to the notion of the class subject. But, on the authors' account,
this was scarcely any longer a structural concept of class. Well
... but it *was* still class! The word, as we know, can be written
with a capital 'c' and behind the definite article. If Laclau and
Mouffe mean to say no more than that class is unimportant, or
at least not so important as Sorel in his way and the Marxists
in theirs understood it to be, or that a confidence in progress
such as Bernstein had is ill-founded, then naturally they have
every right to try to make both the one case and the other, as
indeed any case they may think they can give good reasons to
prove. Their constant cry of 'essentialism', however, evokes some
deeper kind of error, associated with conceptual unity or priority
in themselves. As such, it resembles nothing so much as an obfusca-
tory curse.

Thirdly, in the light of their completed history of Marxism,
we are better placed to judge the claim Laclau and Mouffe make
at the beginning of *Hegemony and Socialist Strategy*, that they 'have
tried to recover some of the variety and richness of Marxist discursivity'.[33] I come back to the matter of richness in just a moment.
As to variety, certainly there is some: Lenin is not Kautsky, Trotsky
and Luxemburg are different from Gramsci, and this is reflected
in what the authors tell us of them. But one is entitled to ask
whether the variety has not proven, in the event, to be of a somewhat superficial kind. From beginning to end, all these writers
were in exactly the same sort of fix, making repeated but vain
attempts to get beyond unity and necessity towards plurality and
contingency. Could a more simplistic story be imagined? One
is not merely entitled but, in the given intellectual context, bound
to ask whether this is not a reduction – of the breadth, the panor-
ama, the continent, of Marxist thought. Laclau and Mouffe may
have happened for once, but this time unwittingly and unwillingly,
upon a genuine 'essentialist' essence: in their own words, when
excoriating 'orthodoxy' for one of its several sins – reduction of
the concrete, be it noted, to the abstract – upon 'an *underlying
reality* to which the ultimate sense of every concrete presence must

necessarily be referred, whatever the level of complexity in the system of mediations.[34] Can a better instance of what they are talking about be cited than the story they have recounted of, and the game they have played with, Marxism? It is hard to think of one. Few, if any, of the Marxists they have taken to task made class so exhaustively the explanation of human existence as they have made 'essentialism' the explanation and meaning of the development of Marxist thought in its entirety.

One bad Althusserian chicken has come home to roost, here, with a vengeance. Whilst putting a considerable intellect at the service of defending historical materialism, Althusser in some ways also showed scant respect, scholarly or just human, for the tradition to which he himself belonged, a great many Marxist lives and ideas; subsuming the specificity and detail of them, their effort to grapple with difficult problems, under a simple, dichotomous division of the intellect and on the wrong side of it. This could not but affect some of those influenced by him and inheriting in a less auspicious political time such easy and too clever disrespect for other Marxisms, both precursive and contemporary. If so many Marxist thinkers, so much of Marxist theorizing, fell beyond the line of intellectual salvation, must that not be because Marxism itself was deficient, inherently? Even in differing from him with this conclusion, they inherited from Althusser, also, something of the passion for closed certainties which he and they liked and like to castigate in others. Only, where he had sought to distinguish just one single, anti-reductionist truth from amongst all the varieties of Marxism, they have found all the varieties of Marxism to be distinct from the one anti-reductionist truth.

A Richness Impoverished

Fourthly, and the crux of the matter, we can see now how Laclau and Mouffe's is an impoverishing account of Marxist thought. To see it in all clarity though, we must look into the face of a conundrum. The two of them think nothing of the logical feat of charging Marxism with being both monist and dualist at the same time. Just where we might have expected a stern 'either ... or', we get a conjunction: monism and dualism both. Actually, the connection is even stronger. More than a conjunction, it is a species of entailment. *Because* it was monist, so the argument is, Marxism has had to be dualist. Unpacking this a bit: because in 'aspiration' or 'profoundly'[35] – let us just say *in essence* – Marxism was monist whilst the world itself was not, Marxist theoreticians trying to come to terms with the world have had to utilize categories extraneous – *really* – to the theory they espoused and become dualists. This describes, once again, an uncomfortable Marxist predicament, a dilemma whose teasing shape we earlier had occasion to notice. Should one make use of any other concepts, then either they are linked 'dialectically' to those of class, the relations of production and so on, and the monism remains unbroken; or they are not thus linked and, consequently, are 'external' to Marxist theory.[36] It is either Kautsky or it is Labriola. The economist rigidity of a Plekhanov may be avoided only for the incoherence of a Gramsci to be the result.[37] Since all the more creative Marxist thinkers have tended towards this latter (dualist) choice, bringing into their discourse a logic of the contingent or idea of the symbolic, as it may be, that was foreign to the basis of their Marxism, it can be said that where the more orthodox were reductionists, the more creative were eclectics. And even they were reductionists. For, at the heart of their eclecticism the reductionism still lurked: in the phrase applied to Gramsci, an 'inner essentialist core';[38] a monism within a dualism. In this place, truly, there can be no salvation, other than by taking leave of Marxism altogether.

But it should be clear, in any event, how the effect of it all is radically to reduce the scope and content, the wealth, of actual Marxist thought: not the shrivelled thing Laclau and Mouffe give out as being its essence; actual Marxist thought as thought by actual Marxists. Much of this has simply been denatured; a whole swathe of arguments, themes, concepts and theory been transmuted and deranged. These are not, as one might previously have thought them, part of the development or deepening, the extension and inner differentiation – part of the richness, precisely – *of* Marxism. They are, so it transpires, incompatible with its monist and reductionist core. Richness of Marxist 'discursivity', therefore, they may be, if the term just refers loosely to the writings of people who happened to be Marxists. But they are a departure, strictly speaking, from Marxist *theory*; so many external supplements more or less *ad hoc*. They betoken not the richness but the poverty of it, and the resulting crisis, the dualism, the incoherence. Now, there is one – very special – angle from which a certain, limited truth can be discerned in this. It is that once Laclau and Mouffe have finished with the concept of hegemony, it is, of course, quite incompatible with any kind of Marxism at all. It has become yet one more representative of an anti-materialist historical outlook in a very long line of them. Not only that: from the vantage point of this new idealism, one can obviously look back over the unfolding Marxist tradition and, so to speak, 'pick out', whether in Luxemburg's thinking on the mass strike, or in Gramsci's concept of hegemony, or in overdetermination (construed as 'constituted in the field of the symbolic'[39]), intellectual features bearing a resemblance of sorts to one's own current beliefs. But this picking out is not a taking or a freeing of what is integrally there, nor the location of genuine points of departure. It is a reading back. For all that it may satisfy some residual loyalty, or assuage a guilt perhaps, towards a now mostly despised intellectual past, it is merely a specimen of those procedures of teleological interpretation which Althusser criticized so effectively in his essay, 'On the Young Marx'.[40] To use a term much employed in *Hegemony and Socialist Strategy*, it is a privileging of the present theoretical moment. Lacking a proper, historical sense of either measure or modesty, this privileging has led here to a view of the whole progression of Marxism since the turn of the century as being preparatory to the advent of Laclau and Mouffe. It is one thing, however, to read all these elements of rich so-called discursivity through the grid of a currently fashionable idea and, seeing them as weak anticipations of it, insightful representatives of a more knowing future, say that they are inconsistent with the Marxism of their authors. To establish in an intellectually cogent way that, in their own place and unadulterated shape, they really were incoherent with Marxist presuppositions, this is something altogether different.

Rosa Luxemburg

Let us consider just one case in a little detail, that of Rosa Luxemburg. It is certainly true that in her thinking on the mass strike Luxemburg puts forward the idea of a generalizing or unifying process, wherein partial conflicts, limited demands, sectional interests, will tend to expand through struggle and merge into a global revolutionary assault.[41] This generalizing tendency, however, is only a summary idea, a brief formula behind which there lie, in her analysis, a whole complex of constituents, causal and experiential. These are at least some of them. First, direct participation in mass struggle is politically educative, there being things which people only learn from their own experience. Second, the collective weight of the proletariat is most effective politically when this class is actually 'assembled as a mass'. Third, a wave of vigorous struggles draws in hitherto unorganized and apolitical sectors of the working class without whose involvement a successful revolution is unthinkable. Fourth, and in consequence of this, such struggles do not endanger or weaken the existing organizations of the labour movement, as is feared by many trade-union bureaucrats; on the contrary, they extend and strengthen them. Fifth – crucially – economic and political dimensions of the overall conflict interact, intersect, run together.[42]

In turn, this fifth point is itself only a concise formula, summing up a series of distinct arguments. How and why do political and economic aspects interact? First, demonstrations or other actions over economic grievances lead to clashes with police or troops, to arrests and deaths, so raising questions about the nature of the state and sparking off actions that are directly political in intent.

Second, in the mass mobilization over economic issues the workers take and exercise in practice political rights, of assembly and free speech, more extensive than they have enjoyed before. Third, the reality and the atmosphere of sharp economic struggles creates a favourable terrain for the influence of social-democratic agitation and political direction. Fourth, the workers derive from these economic conflicts a combativity or 'fighting energy' which is imparted to the field of political battle. Fifth, and in the opposite direction, political rights and freedoms formally gained from the state in consequence of earlier victories can be and are used in the work of strengthening trade-union organization. Sixth, the impetus of national or other large-scale political mobilizations, especially successful ones, is communicated to the more localized and partial economic conflicts as workers, newly encouraged by such successes, become less tolerant of burdensome features of their social condition and take up 'the weapon lying nearest (to) hand'. Seventh, and as a result of this, general political battles sometimes appear to break up and disperse into smaller economic conflicts. Eighth, there is an all-round rise, economic and social, in proletarian conditions of life: better wages and shorter hours provide a basis for intellectual and cultural 'growth'; the despotism of the capitalist is eroded by workplace organization; expectations are aroused which may lead to new struggles if concessions won are subsequently withdrawn – effects all feeding into the further progress of the political struggle.[43]

Different readers will assess this collection of arguments differently and some may want to distinguish amongst them as to the persuasive force of each. However this may be, the important point here is that Luxemburg makes a series of empirical claims and draws a large number of causal and explanatory connections in doing so. One sort of event leads to another sort; this economic cause generates that political effect; a certain political activity or achievement helps, conversely, to strengthen a form of economic organization; a particular type of experience to reinforce commitment or deepen understanding. What do Laclau and Mouffe make of it all? This: 'in a revolutionary situation the *meaning* of every mobilization appears, so to speak, as split: aside from its specific literal demands, each mobilization represents the revolutionary process as a whole; and these totalizing effects are visible in the overdetermination of some struggles by others. This is, however, nothing other than the defining characteristic of the symbol: the overflowing of the signifier by the signified. *The unity of the class is therefore a symbolic unity.*[44] Short work, indeed. Luxemburg, doubt-less, understood something both of the power of symbols and of the symbolic moment in all great mass struggles. But to take her notion that there is a generalizing dynamic within the mass strike and the many hypotheses of fact, cause and effect which this notion embraced, and make them one with the overflowing of the signifier by the signified is a manifest deformation of her own conception. It is an inflation of the symbolic, in line with what *they*, the authors, today believe, but such as reduces that complex of economic, political and intellectual causalities and levels to an interplay of meanings simply, something *she* could not have believed in and in fact did not. If the operation allows Laclau and Mouffe to say that, for Luxemburg, the unity of the class, as also 'the mechanism of unification', is a symbolic one, that is only because they have allowed themselves to 'discover' themselves in her.[45]

Of course, Luxemburg can then be given an intellectual pat on the back for what she has anticipated, but it is one she can do without, mere prelude as it is to the charge of dualism. Assimi-lated to 'a logic of the symbol', 'disruption of every literal meaning' and so on, her 'logic of spontaneism' is now antithetical to that of historical materialism with its 'fixations' of meaning. In a charac-teristic piece of Laclau–Mouffian discourse, the two logics are said to make up a 'double void' (rendered 'invisible' but not 'filled up' by being thought of as 'a confluence of two positive and differ-ent explanatory principles').[46] Whatever may be the interest of this particular claim, however, it is beside the point: irrelevant to showing how, not the logic of the symbol, but Luxemburg's genuine ideas on the mass strike are actually *incompatible* with a Marxist view of history. This is what Laclau and Mouffe need to show and do not. Nor is it clear how they could. Starting – no question about it – from the common structural, or economic, situation of the workers, Luxemburg simply argued that links between them would be forged and tempered, organizations created or strengthened, through a period of vigorous struggle; that they themselves would be educated politically, and the common capacities and weapons they possessed as workers be developed, by mass action. She thereby granted, certainly, significance and effectivity to political and cultural practices. But no good reason has been proposed why her hypotheses about these may not be regarded as complementary to fundamental Marxist principles of class and class interest. None, that is, unless we are to take for one that, irrespective of the theoretical record of actual Marxists, the Marxist paradigm is just 'pre-given' as the narrowest of economisms – as everything here has shown that for Laclau and Mouffe it is. In reality, it is well known, Rosa Luxemburg's mass strike arguments are of a type in no way foreign to Marxist thought. They are as old, generically speaking, as the tradition itself.[47]

Practices of the Game

Considerations of space forbid as detailed a response to *Hegemony and Socialist Strategy*'s other exegeses but one or two brief comments may be offered to supplement the above. Taken as undifferentiated plurality, and of *meanings*, the Althusserian concept of overdetermination is plainly incompatible with giving any kind of explanatory or causal priority to an objective economic structure. Likewise, if a Leninist emphasis on the critical importance of political alliances is seen as the spiritual harbinger of what Laclau and Mouffe for their part will one day mean by hegemony, this is just as incompatible with giving any kind of priority to class. Determination in the last instance by the economy, in the one case, and the fact that Lenin did give priority to class, in the other, can then be made to stand in for economic and class reductionism, the 'in the last instance' and Lenin's emphasis on political alliances (*and* organization and the rest) notwithstanding. You have a dualism. Thus, there is no problem in manipulating concepts so that they come to deputize everywhere for the same two antithetical essences. But what Althusser put forward was neither the single, omnipotent cause nor the mere multiplicity of meanings. It was a conception of the primacy of one type of structure within a group of structures, of a *hierarchy* of causalities of uneven weight. Whatever problems there may be with his central categories, an explanation is needed as to why *this* conception, of a plurality of levels but of differential causal importance, is incoherent and dualist. A more persuasive logic would be required for the purpose than the one we saw brought to bear in the question of relative autonomy and amounting to the assertion, 'Either one is all or all are one.' No other logic is it that dictates that if you think, with Lenin, that political alliances, and therefore politics, are important, you cannot in all consistency think that class, and therefore economic structure, are more fundamentally so; or, by contraposition, that if you do presume to think this, then in effect you reduce politics to being just 'a bare stage' and what have you.[48]

In sum, the perverse entailment, 'monism and, consequently, dualism', simply unravels, and from whichever end one wants. Marxism, according to the authors, is essentially monist and reductionist. From this they infer a dualism, which is to say incoherence, when handling the plain and abundant evidence that much of Marxism is not monist and reductionist. They seek, thus, to neutralize that evidence. But the whole exercise rests on one precarious premiss and this can be denied. Marxism is not *essentially* monist and reductionist. Some Marxisms have tended towards being so and others have not; to the contrary, have taken pains to avoid it. If the premiss is false, no conclusion is derivable from it. Alternatively, and starting at the other end, we may work a contraposition of our own. If the conclusion is false, then so must be the premiss: judging that there are non-reductionist Marxisms which integrate a number of levels or layers of explanation in a coherent

– or, as is in the nature of these things, *more or less* coherent – way, we can affirm of them that, not being dualist, nor therefore are they, covertly, monist.

Let us finish looking at Laclau and Mouffe's treatment of Marxist ideas by just noting a couple of its more bizarre details, subsidiary practices of the game that further testify to the absence here of all sense of reasonable constraint. One such practice may be designated 'moving the goalposts'. Thus, in connection with his views on the exceptional role of the state in pre-revolutionary Russian society, Trotsky is taken to task because, faced with the 'economist' criticisms of the historian Pokrovsky, he 'fails to reply with a theoretical analysis of relative State autonomy in different capitalist social formations, appealing instead to the greenness of life against the greyness of theory.'[49] Now, never mind that the charge is based on nothing more compelling than tendentious quotation, a few lines pulled from an essay of 1922, brief reply to one of Trotsky's critics; that even there, cheek by jowl with those lines, making up the principal emphasis of the reply, there are some half dozen quite explicit formulations of the relative autonomy of the Russian state – 'the relative, that is, historically conditioned and socially limited independence of the autocracy from the ruling classes' – as well as comparative reference in the matter to the states of Western Europe;[50] that Trotsky's full-scale expositions of the theory of permanent revolution, the only basis for a *serious* opinion about this, contain, in the opening chapters of both *Results and Prospects* and *1905*, precisely a theoretical analysis of those factors making for the pronounced autonomy of the Russian state, by comparison and contrast with its European counterparts.[51] Simply leave all this aside. For, though Trotsky could not have known, we do and the authors themselves certainly should know, that the avenue he is upbraided for not having taken is described elsewhere in the book, in relation to other Marxists whom they allow did take it, as 'a dead end'.[52] True, this is later in the book. But a dead end is a dead end, however late in one's discourse one says it. Why Trotsky should be measured by a standard adjudged, itself, to be but another species of Marxist failure is not altogether clear; unless the reason is just that finding any old fault will do.

Then there is the strangely arbitrary – quite difficult to master – practice of adjudicating between different 'essentialisms', displayed, this, in two very short paragraphs in which the relative merits and deficiencies of Bernstein, Sorel and Gramsci are assessed. A mere innocent in these things might imagine that Bernstein and Sorel, actually having broken with Marxism, will possess the advantage. We have already been told of the first of them, after all, that his 'true novelty' was to have recognized 'the autonomy of the political from the economic base'; and of the second ('the most profound and original thinker of the Second International'), that his strength was to have seen that 'social reality itself is indeterminate' – theoretical achievements which even Laclau and Mouffe find it hard to pin on the Marxist, Gramsci, in any straightforward way, and which are central components of their own current viewpoint.[53] Everyone who knows where it's really at these days, though, will know that Gramsci just *has* to win this part of the game: not because he towers over the other two as a thinker; but because, in a certain relevant left milieu, he confers a moral and intellectual legitimacy which they cannot. And this is how it happens. In the first of the two paragraphs, Bernstein is seen off on account of his idea of 'a general law of progress'. Absolute silence for the time being that Gramsci suffers from an 'essentialism' of his own; about him, only good things. In the second paragraph, following as the next one always does just one line later, Gramsci's weakness in that regard *is* mentioned and Sorel therefore given an edge for 'break[ing] more radically than Gramsci with the essentialist vision of *an underlying morphology of history*'.[54] With Bernstein out of the way and seemingly forgotten, this can now be said. Anyway, Sorel has an edge in the one respect only, since, where Gramscian hegemony 'entails the idea of *democratic plurality*, ... the Sorelian myth was simply destined to recreate the unity *of the class*.'[55] Here, something else has been forgotten, albeit from fully five paragraphs previous in the text, something we earlier saw bring Gramsci down. Absolute

silence, in *this* comparison, about 'the unicity of the unifying principle, and its necessary class character'. It is difficult to escape the
feeling of having found that 'space of indeterminacy' in which
more or less anything can be said. This whole procedure too,
however, has a perverse logic to it. The mantle of Gramsci is
vital to a pair of ex-Marxists, so they may represent themselves
as post-Marxists, even while lauding the 'true novelty' of pre-
Marxist ideas.

II

So much, then, for the account we are given of the Marxist tradition. Systematically diminishing as it is, it smooths the way for
the inversion of Althusserian values the authors of *Hegemony and
Socialist Strategy* wish to effect. If Marxist thought now stands against
rather than for a necessary grasp of social complexity, that is
more easily put across by presenting as Marxism what is less than
Marxism, nothing but a wretched travesty in fact. Our survey
of this concluded, we may move on. A deeper source of the same
inversion of values – no justification for the interpretative travesty
but explaining, perhaps, one of the psychological impulses behind
it – lies in the ensemble of ideas for which the Marxist tradition
is here renounced. In the night all cats are grey. Every Marxism,
equally, will seem reductionist from a perspective in which the
spheres of politics and ideology have become superordinate; in
which, more generally, the 'symbolic' has expanded to be all-
encompassing. The break with historical materialism so consum-
mated, giving proper weight, in however measured a way, to history's objective material bases, must look like economism. But
the question once more intrudes itself: why is this perspective
post-Marxist and not the reproduction, as it appears, of something
rather old and familiar? The answer is that it has a more voguish
name; for this is the night of 'discourse'.

Discourse

I have already described the theoretical perspective now defended by Laclau and Mouffe as an idealism. A qualification is in order, however. They themselves do not willingly own to the description. There is, indeed, in their formulation of certain key arguments, an involution of thought and language symptomatic of their reluctance to acknowledge to themselves the simple consequences of the positions they put forward. What we have, therefore, is a shamefaced idealism. Let us look closely at two of its pivotal arguments.

(i) 'Our analysis rejects the distinction between discursive and non-discursive practices. It affirms ... that every object is constituted as an object of discourse, insofar as no object is given outside every discursive condition of emergence.'

(ii) 'The fact that every object is constituted as an object of discourse has *nothing to do* with whether there is a world external to thought, or with the realism/idealism opposition. An earthquake or the falling of a brick is an event that certainly exists, in the sense that it occurs here and now, independently of my will. But whether their specificity as objects is constructed in terms of "natural phenomena" or "expressions of the wrath of God", depends upon the structuring of a discursive field. What is denied is not that such objects exist externally to thought, but *the rather different assertion that they could constitute themselves as objects outside any discursive condition of emergence.*'[56]

About (i) it will suffice to point out that the 'insofar as' clause is mere pleonasm, a repetitition masquerading as a clarification, or elaboration, of the statement it is appended to, and that a possible reason for this linguistic peculiarity is that the statement in question will not readily bear genuine explication without being revealed for the absurdity it is. Every object is constituted as an object of discourse means all objects are given their being by, or are what they are by virtue of, discourse; which is to say (is it not?) that there is no *pre*-discursive objectivity or reality, that objects not spoken, written or thought about *do not exist.* In (ii), the authors appear to step back from this absurdity, denying at first, and emphatically, that it is truly the meaning of what they say. An earthquake exists independently of my will. Very good to hear it, and showing a commendable sense of the real. But this is merely part of the 'now black, now white' style of reasoning commonly to be found in the propagation of what is against all reason and the expression of an all too understandable feeling of intellectual discomfort. Clear signs of warning follow directly on the firm denial. The earthquake's 'specificity' as an object is at once related to a discursive structure, and that in a formula putting back to back the 'constructions' of it as a natural phenomenon and as an act of God; putting on level terms, in other words, what it actually is and a superstition about it. Unless we are to assume Laclau and Mouffe just want to share with their readers the banality that there are different ways of thinking about an earthquake (or: different meanings conferred on it by its articulation within different discursive or symbolic fields), this again seems to suggest that *the sort of object an earthquake is*, not therefore merely the idea, but the reality of it, is determined by discourse. The concluding sentence of (ii) then sews up the whole 'yea and nay' argument good and proper. Once more the authors step back from the absurd: what is denied is not that objects exist externally to thought but a 'rather different' assertion. It is indeed rather different, but mainly – in fact, only – by being nicely obscure. Could an earthquake 'constitute itself as an object outside any discursive condition of emergence'? Leaving aside the eccentricity of expression which has an earthquake constituting itself, the only sensible answer to the question is: yes – if one does not think, for example, that earthquakes would cease to happen should humanity perish. But Laclau and Mouffe say no; this is exactly what they have been careful to specify as the true content of their denial.

A few lines later in their text all confusion is resolved, any lingering doubt over the meaning I have construed from the two quoted passages laid to rest. We learn here finally that 'the very classical dichotomy between an objective field constituted outside of any discursive intervention and a discourse consisting of the pure expression of thought' has been overtaken within 'several currents of contemporary thought'.[57] One need not accept the loaded way in which the second part of this distinction is formulated – for no discourse is *purely* thought – in order to insist that the first part of it is an absolutely indispensable principle, whether or not the authors still consider it to be 'in'. However frequently these may be denied, either in high philosophical argument or in popular assertion, a pre-discursive reality and an extra-theoretical objectivity form the irreplaceable basis of all rational enquiry, as well as the condition of meaningful communication across and between differing viewpoints. This foundation once removed, one simply slides into a bottomless, relativist gloom, in which opposed discourses or paradigms are left with no common reference point, uselessly trading blows. The most elementary facts of existence become strictly unthinkable without the aid of more or less elaborate theoretical sophistries. Was not the pre-human world 'an objective field constituted outside of any discursive intervention' – or did it have to await the appearance of humanity to 'construct' it? And *even* today, 'several currents of contemporary thought' notwithstanding, are there not realities of nature, both external and human, which are not merely 'given outside' every discourse (see (i)) but the material precondition of them all? Refuse this, anyway, who will. As a certain Marxist 'essentialist' long ago said, 'Once you deny objective reality ... you have already lost every weapon against fideism.'[58]

Laclau and Mouffe go on to repeat their contention about the aforesaid dichotomy in slightly different terms. 'The main consequence of a break with the discursive/extra-discursive dichotomy,' they argue, 'is the abandonment of the thought/reality opposition.' So much for the claim that all this has 'nothing to do' with whether there is a world external to thought, and with the realism/idealism distinction (see (ii)). For, a world well and truly *external* to thought obviously has no meaning outside the thought/reality opposition. And purporting to have gone beyond that opposition, apart from being, itself, a *very* old story, is precisely one of idealism's most typical forms. Its role, in the present instance, this supposed going beyond, is to mask from the authors the last absurd consequences, whose naked visage they plainly fear to see exposed, of the belief they have chosen to make their own: that all the world is discourse.[59]

Hegemonic Articulation

Since our primary interest, however, is the sort of social and political theory this belief sustains, we may put the question of earthquakes behind us. We must examine the notion of *hegemonic articulation*, crux of what *Hegemony and Socialist Strategy* has to offer: a notion of the bringing together in a common formation or ensemble, and through discursive practices of politics and ideology, of diverse identities or subject positions, social sectors, movements and struggles. We may begin by laying out some basic definitions and theses. The authors 'call *articulation* any practice establishing a relation among elements such that their identity is modified as a result of the articulatory practice.' A distinction is proposed in this context between two kinds of entity: on the one hand, 'moments', whose identity is defined by their position within the 'structured totality' – or discourse – 'resulting from the articulatory practice'; on the other hand, 'elements', which are constituted independently of it.[60] I return to this distinction shortly. The concept of hegemony, for its part, 'supposes a theoretical field dominated by the category of *articulation*.'[61] It supposes, that is to say, a terrain that is *open* to these articulatory practices because marked by that disparateness, complexity and plurality which are their raw materials, which make them possible at all. A terrain already unified around some central essence, a closed or a sutured totality, would leave no room for such practices. The requisite 'openness' here, therefore, is the one we are familiar with, 'the incomplete and open character of the social'. This 'openness of the social is ... the precondition of every hegemonic practice.'[62]

It is acceptable to speak of a 'hegemonic *subject*' and of 'the subject of any articulatory practice',[63] but not in the sense of a constitutive or founding agent. 'Whenever we use the category of "subject" in this text,' Laclau and Mouffe write, 'we will do so in the sense of "subject positions" within a discursive structure. Subjects cannot, therefore, be the origin of social relations – not even in the limited sense of being endowed with powers that render an experience possible – as all "experience" depends on precise discursive conditions of possibility.'[64] Much the same can be said in the case of other important categories. Thus, 'every social identity' is 'the meeting point for a multiplicity of articulatory practices'.[65] And the direction or meaning of any 'social struggle', any 'movement', depends 'upon its forms of articulation within a given hegemonic context', or again, 'upon its hegemonic articulation with other struggles and other demands'.[66] We do not just look out, though, on a sort of ceaseless, uncatchable, discursive flux, mere featureless plurality of articulatory practices. The very idea of hegemony implies otherwise. 'Any discourse is constituted as an attempt to dominate the field of discursivity, to arrest the flow of differences, to construct a centre.' The 'privileged discursive points' that result from such attempts are called 'nodal points', and there can be 'a variety of hegemonic nodal points' in any 'social formation'.[67]

Hegemonic practices 'operate in political fields crisscrossed by antagonisms'. Indeed, 'the two conditions of a hegemonic articulation are the presence of antagonistic forces and the instability of the frontiers which separate them. Only the presence of a vast area of floating elements and the possibility of their articulation to opposite camps – which implies a constant redefinition of the latter – is what constitutes the terrain permitting us to define a practice as hegemonic.' The existence of 'two camps', where this comes about, is itself an effect and not a condition of hegemonic articulation. For, it is not 'a dichotomically divided political space' but rather a 'proliferation of ... political spaces' that is 'a central characteristic of the advanced capitalist social formations'. It has been so since 'the beginning of modern times, when the reproduc-

tion of the different social areas takes place in permanently changing conditions'.[68]

Now, even on the basis of what we have so far, there is much
upon which comment might be passed. One could note again,
for instance, how absolutely everything – subjects, experience,
identity, struggles, movements – has discursive 'conditions of possibility', while the question as to what might be the conditions of
possibility of discourse itself does not trouble the authors so much
as to pause for thought. *These* conditions can be passed over in
a parenthetical phrase, only to be cancelled out. Thus, because
all experience depends on 'precise' discursive conditions, subjects
are no kind of social 'origin', 'not even in the limited sense of
being endowed with powers that render an experience possible'.
The stroke of logic involved in this bears some scrutiny, at least
by those who have an interest in the rhetoric of false argument.
What it amounts to is: because d is a condition of e, one can
deny that p is also a condition of e, even if p *is* also a condition
of e.[69] We are confronted, in fact, and predictably enough given
the way in which our simple – natural – earthquake was discursively gobbled up, with an overweening *social ontology*, itself without
conditions, unlimited, unquestionable. In these respects, at any
rate, it is not dissimilar to the Althusserian conceptual universe,
populated by decree, from end to end, with 'practices'. As one
of Althusser's early critics aptly wrote, 'It "happens" that everything is production. ... That is how it is.' So, too, it just 'happens'
in the present case, but this time with discourse.[70]

Between Elements and Moments

I want to concentrate critical attention, however, on two matters.
In doing so, I shall seek to lay bare the intellectual vacuity of
what Laclau and Mouffe put forth. Borrowing the expression with
which they themselves favour Rosa Luxemburg, though trying
to show that it has a force here which it lacked applied to her,
I shall argue that at the heart of their book there is a 'double

void': double, because empty, equally, of theoretical substance and of any genuine practico-normative specificity or direction.

Our point of access to the theoretical 'side' of this void is the distinction between elements and moments. Let us see what light it throws on the notion of hegemonic articulation. When considering the various subject positions, social identities, struggles and so forth which any particular practice of hegemonic articulation puts into relation, what sort of entities are we dealing with and what is the nature of the ensemble they collectively compose? If this were to be thought of as a mere combination of *elements*, then by the distinction proffered their identity would be given *independently* of the articulatory practice itself and the relations between them, therefore, be *external* relations and purely *contingent*. Alternatively, if it were conceived as a structure or totality of *moments*, then the identity or meaning of these would be determined by their *place within* the articulated ensemble, thus by their relations to one another, and such relations be both *internal* and *necessary* ones. The choice, so defined, poses a difficulty of which Laclau and Mouffe are well aware. Neither alternative, in fact, will do.

For, to opt for the first would be to saddle onself with 'essentialist fixity'.[71] This comes upon people in a thousand different guises. There is not only, as we already know, an 'essentialism of the totality', there is also an 'essentialism of the elements'; and nothing is to be gained by replacing the one with the other. So, a 'conception which denies any essentialist approach to social relations, must also state the precarious character of every identity and the impossibility of fixing the sense of the "elements" in any ultimate literality.'[72] A heavy charge brought against the Marxist tradition, it will be remembered, was that where it recognized the importance of class alliances, it conceived these as mere relations of exteriority between independent agents of determinate identity. But 'the very identity of classes is transformed by the hegemonic tasks they take on themselves ... the notion of "class alliance" is ... clearly insufficient, since hegemony supposes the construction of the very identity of social agents, and not just a rationalist coincidence of "interests" among preconstituted agents.'[73] The same, we have seen, goes for the meaning of all movements and struggles; and, as for any hegemonic task, 'its identity is given to it solely by its articulation within a hegemonic formation.' The first alternative, then, is no good, just 'a new form of fixity: that of the various decentred subject positions'.[74] It might appear to point us, by its deficiencies, towards the second alternative: that the hegemonic ensemble is a structure or totality of moments.

But that is no good, either. It would be a form of closure, simply one more sutured totality, with the hegemonic formation itself now conceptualized 'as founding totality of its partial processes'.[75] If the idea of such a closure has been renounced for society as a whole – which is the meaning, incidentally, of the recurring formulations, 'the impossibility of the object "society"', ' "Society" is not a valid object of discourse', ' "society" is impossible', 'the impossibility of "society"'[76] – this is because it is renounced for the generality of the social, hence with respect to *every* social ensemble, large or small. It cannot be readmitted even to a more reduced social space without overturning the hallowed principle of anti-'essentialism'. The very category of articulation would be placed in jeopardy by that. Nothing would be solved 'if the relational and differential logic of the discursive totality prevailed without any limitation. In that case, we would be faced with pure relations of necessity, and ... any articulation would be impossible given that every "element" would *ex definitione* be "moment".' As the authors also put it, 'if articulation is a practice ... it must imply some form of separate presence of the elements which that practice articulates or recomposes.'[77] This might appear, in turn, to point us back to the first alternative. But we have already been there and it led us here. We want the exit, if there is one, from an endlessly looping circularity.

And there is one. It is, at first sight, a model of elegant simplicity. The various constituents of a hegemonic formation are neither elements nor moments; they are something in between. Their status, according to Laclau and Mouffe, 'is constituted in some intermediate region between the elements and the moments.' This region, in which the 'transition from the "elements" to the "moments" is never entirely fufilled', is also referred to, at one point, as a 'no-man's land'.[78] In fact, it is a marsh. The type of coherence characteristic of the hegemonic ensemble, distinct at once from that of a combination of elements and from that of a totality of moments, is designated by the concept of 'regularity in dispersion', and the beauty of this concept is that it allows you to say exactly what you want. It endows the articulated formation with just enough internality, so to speak, that you can rail against all fixity and exteriority of social identities with respect to one another when it suits you to do this; but not so much internality as will comprehensively suture that formation or prevent you from... *affirming* some fixity and separateness of social identities when it suits you to do that. The concept of 'regularity in dispersion' is tailor-made for facing all ways simultaneously.[79] Here are some examples of how it works.

Take, first, 'fixity'. This has been a key target of *Hegemony and Socialist Strategy* and, in the strictures they address to Marxist thinkers, the authors are very firm about it. 'Unfixity,' they say, 'has become the condition of every social identity.' A break with 'orthodox essentialism' must entail 'the critique of *every type of fixity*, through an affirmation of the incomplete, open and politically negotiable character of every identity'.[80] But if there were truly *no* fixity, thoroughgoing social indeterminacy and that is all, there would be nothing more of consequence for the putative social theorist to say, a fact which Laclau and Mouffe have duly to acknowledge, with the concession, 'a discourse incapable of generating any fixity of meaning is the discourse of the psychotic.' The polemical moment of their enterprise behind them and the constructive moment once begun, it turns out that 'neither absolute fixity nor absolute non-fixity is possible'. *Some* fixity, then, is all right after all.[81] So it is with other pertinent categories. External relations, as between discrete social agents or struggles, have been severely criticized where Marxism was concerned and the constitutive, meaning-giving powers of hegemonic articulation asserted repeatedly against them. But then it comes about that these powers do not actually prevail 'without limitation by any exterior'. No, there is an 'irresoluble interiority/exteriority tension'; 'neither a total interiority nor a total exteriority is possible'.[82] The same applies to necessity and contingency, that two-pronged stick wielded by Laclau and Mouffe to discomfort every writer whom they suspected of having toyed with it. More adept with the distinction themselves, they inform us, now, that 'necessity only exists as a partial limitation of the field of contingency'; and, also, that this relationship 'cannot be conceived as ... between two areas that are delimited and external to each other ... because the contingent only exists within the necessary.'[83] No question here, in any case, of a baleful 'dualism'. Society, finally, may be impossible, as we are told half a dozen times, but discursive practices nevertheless have a stab at this impossibility by way of the structured totalities they severally articulate, and the effort is not altogether in vain. For, some fixity means some closure and some closure, obviously, a qualification of the much-emphasized 'openness'. So: 'If society is not totally possible, neither is it totally impossible.'[84]

It seems appropriate at this point to remind the reader of the sharp alternatives with which Marxism was confronted. But here everything is permitted. It is perhaps not surprising, in the light of it all, that the authors themselves say of hegemony, at one place, that it is 'a type of relation that never manages to be identical with itself'; and again, in the flourish that concludes their book, that it is a 'game' which 'eludes the concept'. That expresses a deep, though probably unintended, truth about *Hegemony and Socialist Strategy*.[85]

A Theoretical Void

To guard against one possible misunderstanding in this matter: it is not a question of wanting to impose on Laclau and Mouffe the sort of rigid choice they freely impose on others, by insisting in our turn that the identities and so forth which any hegemonic politics articulates must *either* be elements *or* be moments. If they would rather have them in between, so be it. These are then *modified elements*, their character and meaning constituted *in part* independently of the hegemonic political project itself and *in part* by the effects of this project upon them. That may not yet say very much but it does say something. Three observations are in order, however. First, some consistency and precision of usage is required. If this is how it is, then this is how it is, an 'intermediacy' between elements and moments; and one cannot therefore just play each end against the other, now speaking as if we had pure moments, and now as if simple independent elements, according to convenience. But that is exactly what Laclau and Mouffe do, and they do it not only before introducing us to that 'no-man's land' in which all antinomies are renegotiated, but also afterwards. Thus, when they want, in their final chapter, to emphasize the virtues of pluralism against any domineering Marxist ambition, they tell us that 'pluralism is *radical* only to the extent that each term of this plurality of identities finds within itself the principle of its own validity', and talk accordingly of 'the autoconstitutivity of each one of its terms' – a bit fixed and separate, one might think. Then, when it is the rights of hegemonic articulation that are to the fore again, which happens soon enough, we learn: 'there are hegemonic practices because this radical unfixity' – unscathed; despite the renegotiation – 'makes it impossible to consider the political struggle as a game in which the identity of the opposing forces is constituted from the start. .. If the meaning of each struggle is not given from the start, this means that it is fixed – partially – only to the extent that the struggle moves outside itself and ... links itself structurally to other struggles.' Black on the heels of white: and each way '*only* to the extent that'. The circle remains in place.[86]

Second, the resounding hollowness of the critique of Marxism we have been offered is now exposed beneath its shell of words. Taxed many times over with conceiving social identities as constituted, or 'fixed', external to the – hegemonic – political project itself, Marxist politics has been asked to make way for a more authentic hegemonic, and radical, politics; only to find that this

107

too, by its very nature as an articulatory practice, presupposes a certain fixity and exteriority of identities, 'some form of separate presence of the elements', amongst its conditions.[87] The difference, we will be told, is that in this case the fixity and externality are 'discursively constructed' ones. But that is just another circle. It was fixity and 'external alliances' that were the sins of Marxism, and gainsaying them the apparent virtues of the proffered discourse theory. The argument looks somewhat different if it is only that the fixations external to any hegemonic politics are conceived by this *discourse* theory as – discursive. This throws us back on the idealist ontology pure and simple, and we have seen how feeble is the case which has been made for that. Or, it will be said, your (Marxist, 'classist', etc.) fixations are absolute ones, whereas ours are only partial and relative. But if the distinction is anything more than a coded repetition of the argument just dismissed, it rests upon the travesty of Marxism we earlier criticized: that it is a reductionism for which politics and ideology do not *really* count.

Third, this whole notion of hegemonic articulation, with its region intermediate between the elements and the moments: how much *does* it in fact say? We know from it that there is a plurality and variety of subject positions, all discursively constituted, that some of them can become the source of hegemonic practices – though none of them is structurally 'privileged' in this respect, the thing depending on 'a political initiative'[88] – that these practices in turn modify their component elements and therefore subject positions, articulating and articulated alike, and succeed, some of them, in establishing hegemonic nodal points. What else? And does this knowledge help us to understand or explain anything *specific* at all? Are some hegemonic practices, for example, more likely than others to prevail, or to prevail in certain conditions, and if so, why or in what conditions? Would it be due only, or mainly, to the inherent 'attractiveness' of the discourses in play and, if so, what might be the criteria of *that*, given that any adjudication between discourses is itself another discourse, with no more purchase on an impossible objectivity than they? Would it have anything to do with material or other resources in different subject positions? Or with differential political capacities (and what would be the reason for these)? Would it depend on already existing structures, political or other, and if so, what would be the nature and scope of this dependence? Or must we just assume that openness and indeterminacy of the social mean, here, such a free play of discourses and articulatory practices that *any number* of outcomes is always possible, so that no particular outcome, no specificity, *can* be understood or explained? Whatever is, then, simply is, but, whatever it is, it can always be subsumed under the (re)description of the social world as a discursive plurality with some nodal points. It is hard to see how one could get any closer to complete theoretical vacuity.

By way of possible response, in any case, to questions of the above sort, Laclau and Mouffe offer next to nothing. I say 'next to' nothing because there is one gesture, and there are some strange apparitions, which may be considered relevant. The former consists of a bare announcement, at a couple of places, that not everything is possible, that the play or the flow of discursive practices is not entirely free (only free − of course! − 'of any a priori class character of struggles or demands'), that there *are* some 'limits'.[89] A qualification of total indeterminacy, this remains merely a gesture, however, because, unelaborated, it actually furnishes none of the desiderata of explanatory specificity, only promises some. As for the strange apparitions, these tend to pop up suddenly whenever the authors want to put something with a little more historical content into the empty shell of their own version of hegemony. We then get: 'advanced capitalism', 'the advanced capitalist social formations' and 'the social formation as an empirical referent' (sic); 'the capitalist periphery' and 'imperialist exploitation'; 'an intensive regime of accumulation', 'commodification'; and so on.[90] Is it necessary to say that these concepts belong to another theory? Nor is it clear what they are doing here: where society is not 'totally possible'; where objective interests have no theoretical basis; and economism, or even the 'core' of it, is to be avoided at all costs. So is this a case of untamed 'survivals'?

Or is it a case, rather, of needing concepts for what 'discourse' has banished, whenever reality intrudes upon the game? Or is it that, as the Introduction to *Hegemony and Socialist Strategy* barely hints, Marxist categories may still possess a 'degree of validity' – despite everything?[91] Whatever the case, poor Bernstein, though: again forgotten. For allowing *something* to those categories, he was guilty of a dualism.[92] Our authors are allowed whatever they may need on the given page.

Progressivity without Foundations

We may proceed now to the other, the practico-normative, 'side' of the double void their book contains. It can be located by considering just where, in all this, there is a basis for any *particular* political direction or orientation. Laclau and Mouffe will occasionally make use of a term like 'progressive', and seemingly align themselves with it, as they do with the project of the 'left', or, at least, of 'a new left'.[93] But what can 'progressive' mean for them? Of course, we all do have some rough and ready idea of its meaning, but that is because it forms part of certain established discourses – socialist, liberal, humanist, rationalist, and so on – in the context of which one can, with a little thought and analysis, identify its specific sense or senses. But one is not entitled simply to presume upon these discourses and deploy meanings that are parasitic on them, if, as is the case with the authors, one has rejected the very assumptions there that underpin these meanings. It does not seem a lot to ask of a book so obsessed with the constitution and fluctuation of all symbolic values that it should interrogate, and reflect upon, the content of such 'uni-directional' normative terms as it is willing to inherit.

Three standard possible bases of a putatively 'progressive' (or left) orientation are not available to Laclau and Mouffe. One is the notion of objective interests, satisfaction of which might serve as an index of social progress. The exercise of attributing these to social agents has been dubbed 'arbitrary' and the notion itself dismissed as being 'eschatological'. A second is 'reference to any *general* principle or substratum of an anthropological nature' – the 'anthropological assumption of a "human nature"' – and by implication, therefore, any conception of essential human qualities and needs. As is to be expected in a post-structuralist terrain, this sort of foundation for a meaning of progressivity is given short shrift. ' "Man" is a discursively constructed subject position', it is asserted, and the range of its possible articulations 'infinite'. The only argument, if such it can be called, for the alleged infinitude is that a human 'essence' would be 'presumably a gift from heaven', the authors carefully ignoring alternative sources closer to the ground.[94] Thirdly, a concept of exploitation or something similar, in which trans-historical principles of justice or fairness are either explicit or presupposed, is also not a viable option. True, Laclau and Mouffe express themselves in favour of normative analysis and discussion involving 'justice' amongst other things. But it is clear, when they do so, that uppermost in their minds is a current *political* consideration: that of putting a healthy distance between themselves and so-called 'classism'.[95] A theoretical perspective in which 'the era of universal discourses' has 'come to an end', can have no more room for a trans-historical, universalist notion of justice than it can for the concept of a universal human nature – always assuming some minimal effort of intellectual consistency.[96] Where, then, is the basis, or a meaning, for a direction we could call progressive; where, indeed, the basis for a specific direction of any kind?

A merely apparent basis is tendered to us in the definitions the authors give of subordination and oppression. 'We shall understand by a *relation of subordination* that in which an agent is subjected to the decisions of another – an employee with respect to an employer, for example, or in certain forms of family organization the woman with respect to the man, and so on. We shall call *relations of oppression*, in contrast, those relations of subordination which have transformed themselves into sites of antagonisms.' So,

111

the subordination of slaves becomes an oppression if and when the relationship to the slave-holder becomes an antagonistic one, and the subordination of women likewise when feminism, as a movement against it, has the same 'antagonizing' effect.[97] Commonsensical and obvious as these definitions may seem at first sight, they are in fact completely useless, only gaining what semblance of plausibility they have from the examples appended to them. For, one is 'subjected to the decisions', on a perfectly regular basis, of all sorts of people: as, for example, of bus conductors, with regard to deportment on the bus; of neighbours, in respect of the kinds of exterior and garden and car they oblige you to see; and – in case that should seem footling – of employees, if you have them and they belong to a strong trade union; of democratic majorities, if you are a member, say, of some radical rightist minority which does not believe in democracy.

Let us now put this observation together with the notion of 'antagonism', since it is that which transforms subordination into downright oppression. I shall leave aside the fact that Laclau and Mouffe have themselves earlier argued, or at least appeared to argue, that this notion defies precise definition, 'escapes the possibility of being apprehended through language';[98] because what it actually comes down to is that a relation of subordination becomes an antagonism and hence an oppression when the discourse (or discourses) by which it is constructed is (or are) challenged by other discourses, when there is 'a discursive "exterior" from which the discourse of subordination can be interrupted'. The position of a slave is rendered an antagonistic one only in terms of a discursive formation, such as that of human rights, in which the subordination can be 'constructed as oppression'.[99] One may note how this completely relativizes what counts as oppression, so that a young child, for instance, cut off from all social contact, beaten and tormented, bewildered and without the concepts of any other 'legitimacy' than that of her tormentors, could not be said to be oppressed. But equally to the point here are the cases of people who will, now, be oppressed: a householder sponsoring the discourse that no one is entitled to impose the sight of an unkempt garden on those around them, and unlucky, in this respect, in the neighbours he has; capitalists firm in the conviction that trade unions ought to be outlawed; and so on. Slavery, apartheid, concentration camps, are all instances of oppression (when they are), and so too are cases like these.

This inference from the definitions tendered is so outlandish as to give rise to the suggestion that it cannot be what Laclau and Mouffe really mean. There are two possible responses to that suggestion. One is that it is up to them to say what they mean and this is *what they say*, together with some straightforward, unstrained derivations from it. A second, more charitable, response would be: quite so – this is probably not what they really mean. But, then, what do they mean? In fact, their definitions and examples of subordination and oppression trade on unspoken assumptions concerning *illicit power* or inequalities which are unjust, 'brutal',[100] or unacceptable in some other way. Illicit, unjust, brutal or unacceptable, however, according to what standard? By locating the meaning of oppression within so many discourses of mere antagonism and thereby scattering it to the four winds, they have robbed themselves of the very criteria they need here: objectivist, universal, or just plain determinate. Either way, therefore, whichever response is preferred, we are left with a normative vacuum. If we take the authors at their word, their concepts of subordination and oppression can supply no useful index of what is progressive, since the breadth of the first and the fluidity implicit in the second combine to merge together the ugly realities of real human oppression with mere vexations, cases of special pleading, the defence, even, of exploitation and privilege. And if we do not take them at their word, we are forced back upon the principles of *other* theories than their own, principles they have summarily rejected. Untroubled by the consciousness of any problem, Laclau and Mouffe may be happy on occasion to speak of 'the *arbitrary character* of a whole set of relations of subordination' being '*laid bare*'.[101] But the kinds of normative foundation which would give sense, and specific content, to this judgement are precisely the ones they have forsworn.

Arbitrariness

The true arbitrariness, therefore, is that which the discourse of *Hegemony and Socialist Strategy* itself establishes and merely another face of the omnipresent 'indeterminacy'. It is hardly to be wondered at that this ends up producing a theoretical construct which could support *any* kind of politics. The authors themselves *say* – over and again – radical democracy, a point I return to presently. But why it should be that and a broadly 'progressive' politics rather than something of a different, and reactionary, stripe; why such-and-such a discursive or hegemonic practice and not some other should be deemed worthy of any commitment; is unexamined and, in terms of their own theoretical categories, unfounded. That, simply, is how it is: one choice – a leap? – amongst a multiplicity of divergent discourses. Symptomatic in this regard is a passage in which Laclau and Mouffe reflect upon the political significance of Sorel's ideas. The anti-economist and 'mythic' emphases there, they acknowledge, led some of his followers to nationalism and thence to fascism. But it was, they argue, only one possible direction. He was also influential in the formation of Gramsci's thought, and the very perception of social indeterminacy that was his strength, though it could lead some to fascism, could lead in other directions as well; such as Bolshevism which Sorel himself enthusiastically welcomed. This 'indeterminacy' of direction is clearly offered to us as a form of reassurance. What is more puzzling is why it should be seen as reassuring, about a given set of ideas, that it can take those who subscribe to them just about anywhere.[102]

I shall bring the case I have sought to make about the double void here to a conclusion with one other observation about arbitrariness. It is not difficult to project how Laclau and Mouffe, who have turned a *certain* (bad) Althusserian practice against its progenitor, could themselves be outdone by someone impressed by their methods of advocacy. For, these methods amount, as I have said, to this: that resort to any unifying principle(s) of explanation can be criticized and dismissed as an 'essentialism'. But it is in the nature of writing intelligibly and to some purpose that one imposes or tries to discover *some* kind of order. And even they, though their prose is in places impenetrably opaque, and for all the fudging and self-contradiction they go in for, and despite the hollowness of what they finally have to offer, do this. Their first and their last thought mere disparateness, plurality, they need, no less than we, a framework, a degree of order, some fixity, and so they have them: everything is discourse and the discursive is everywhere, such determinations as there are deriving from that. Well, then? 'They failed to recognize that here, compromising their bold venture towards a logic of contingency for the non-sutured space of the social, was just one more essence; behind disparateness, Discourse; reductive abstract within the manifold concrete; even in its protestations of openness, a new form of monist closure' — and so forth. The game is easily played and easily turned. 'Discourse', too, can be written with a capital 'd'. A *total* nihilism, unqualified chaos of factors and types — discourses, yes, but also other things of an inexhaustible, ineffable diversity — presumably follows. One may hope, however, to be spared this last deconstructive step. No matter what theoretical form it might take, it would be, in practical, political terms, pointless. Laclau–Mouffian indeterminacy, though a little way short of such 'completion', already yields the unfounded — arbitrary — choice of more or less whatever politics you want.

'Democratic Imaginary'

It remains only to make some comment on the sort of politics the authors themselves plump for, pluralist–democratic, beyond 'classism', and striking, withal, some of the all too familiar notes of the newly virtuous ex-Marxist. On democracy, I shall confine myself to two points, otherwise just referring readers to Ellen Meiksins Wood's excellent critique of the theme's treatment in *Hegemony and Socialist Strategy*.[103] I preface them, however, by saying that I take it as *axiomatic* that socialism must be democratic, and neither

115

point represents any departure from that. There is much more
that needs to be said about it, of course, but reaffirmation of
the axiom is necessary here because, though one might not guess
this from Laclau and Mouffe's book, it has been a *fundamental*
and a *common* conviction of *very many Marxists of the last two decades*,
inside that broad (and pluralistic) intellectual current to which
the two of them have now bid such a shoddy farewell. It could
be so, moreover, because none of us had to start from scratch;
we could build on the experience of earlier generations of Marxists,
renowned thinkers and rank-and-file activists alike. We knew –
what the authors have evidently forgotten – and sought to
strengthen and extend, the principles and sources within the
Marxist tradition which, against both the forms and the pretensions
of 'actually existing socialism', spoke insistently of socialist democracy: in Marx, from his earliest philosophical writings to the Paris
Commune; in Trotsky, from the pluralist arguments of *Our Political
Tasks* to the fight against Stalinism; in Luxemburg – incandescent
– practically everywhere; *and* in Lenin, and elsewhere besides.
The cover of darkness, either intellectual or contemporary–political, was not a necessary excuse.

In any case, as to the first point, Laclau and Mouffe's text
is liberally sprinkled with phrases of the sort, 'more free, democratic
and egalitarian societies', 'the project of a radical democracy',
'a radical, libertarian and plural democracy', 'a pluralist and
democratic conception', 'a radical and plural democracy'.[104] Given
that they also make reference to socialism's negative record in
this regard, to the point of suggesting that democracy has hitherto
been foreign to socialism, one might have expected some elaboration of their own 'radical' democratic conception: something
about institutional forms and procedures, structures and levels
of representation, constitutional norms, and so on. In fact, there
is under this heading but a single sentence. 'The forms of democracy should therefore also be plural, inasmuch as they have to
be adapted to the social spaces in question – direct democracy
cannot be the only organizational form, as it is only applicable
to reduced social spaces.'[105] That is all. For the rest, this virtual

116

absence of institutional specification meets a need for them that must be met for every rightward-moving Marxist or ex-Marxist current. This is the need, while rightly emphasizing some continuity of *forms* and *procedures* between existing and projected democracies, to maintain a critical silence about necessary discontinuities, so lending credence, if not outright allegiance, to the eternal legitimacy claimed by the existing *state*.

The second point is that for all their criticism of Marxism's multiple simplifications, the authors themselves present a breathtakingly simple account of modern history. It can be summed up in a phrase: the extension of the democratic idea (or 'democratic imaginary' in their own parlance).[106] Born of the French Revolution and initially bringing with it a civil and political equality, it was then extended to struggles and demands over economic relations – which is why socialism is 'a moment internal to the democratic revolution'[107] – then by feminism to gender relations, and so on. Whether or not the accumulated wealth of Marxist historiography need have anything to fear from historical explanation such as this, I shall take the risk of labouring a point by saying that it does look, again, remarkably like an 'essentialist' origin or centre – and like the progressive unfolding of the Idea, at that.[108]

As for the 'retreat from class', this is undoubtedly where the potential appeal of *Hegemony and Socialist Strategy* lies and it will be responsible for whatever political resonance the book turns out to have. A would-be philosophy for contemporary, or new, social movements and struggles, it is overtly addressed to the variety of their concerns, whether of gender or ethnicity, ecology, nuclear power, war and peace.[109] It is perhaps unnecessary to linger over one obvious consequence of the foregoing critique, if this has any force: namely, that those for whom such are, quite properly, serious concerns would be wise to look elsewhere for a philosophical charter or theoretical basis – whatever their judgement of the strengths, weaknesses and theoretical potentialities of Marxist thought. There is a difference between providing a theory of, and for, these movements and struggles, something of intellectual rigour and substance, and simply leaning on them to gain support for a flaccid pose. It will bear repeating on Marxism's behalf, in this matter and these times, that though it has always viewed both the working class and the abolition of capitalist exploitation as strategically decisive to the goal of human emancipation, it set its face also from the very beginning against all forms of oppression, sexual, national, racial and religious, as well as economic. In that sense, it *was* and *is*, proudly and self-consciously so in the persons of its most clear-sighted representatives, a discourse of tendentially *universal* scope.[110] The actual record, whether of Marxist theories or Marxist organizations, has often fallen far short of the broad aspiration, though this *too* can be simplified, to the extent even of becoming a reactionary falsehood; and Marxism has always had, and still has, a lot to learn from other, non-Marxist theories and outlooks. But if it is not a closed or final truth and must know how to live with a political and intellectual pluralism, it is also the case that any putatively radical discourse that just turns its back on Marxism will quickly reach its limits, limits continually recreated by capitalism and class. Worse still, if it should bend towards an easy and fashionable anti-Marxism.

For Laclau and Mouffe today, it is no longer possible to regard the working class as having a special, or 'privileged', connection with the struggle for socialism. They do allow, it is true, that there is no incompatibility here. But a fundamental interest in socialism is not deducible from any economic position: 'there is no logical connection whatsoever between positions in the relations of production and the mentality of the producers.' Other 'democratic antagonisms', what is more, are *'on an equal footing'* with proletarian ones in this regard. '[P]olitical practice constructs the interests it represents.'[111] If the argument were only that workers are not automatically, and by virtue simply of being workers, socialists, the authors should have saved themselves the trouble of it. The suggestion, however, that there is no stronger relation between socialism and the working class than there is between socialism and anybody else is an idealism – or indeterminacy, if one so prefers – run wild. The cavalier disregard it displays, in the name of discourse, for material realities, relationships and needs may be gauged by trying out the same sort of argument, as Laclau and Mouffe conveniently do not, on another pertinent 'subject position'. Could it conceivably be supposed that feminist discourses and struggles have no more particular connection with one kind of social agent than with any other? Or do they, rather, especially concern and involve women, basic source both of their existence and of their vigour? And is this not in consequence of *objective* features of the economic and social position of women? Here as elsewhere, material structures and determinants shape and limit what political practice can 'construct'. If socialism *is* still envisaged, internal moment of the democratic revolution or not, then the specific relation, of exploitation, that is *definitive of what capitalism is* still has to be abolished; and it is a mere fancy to think that the social agent subordinated by this relation could be anything but central to the project of its abolition.

The Ex-Marxist's Conscience

I shall conclude by simply registering some of the more lamentable themes of this book from professed (and so-recently-Marxist) radicals; themes which give reason to ponder just how far 'post-' is from straightforward *anti*-Marxism. First, there is deployment of a concept of 'totalitarianism' in its familiar Cold War sense as denoting something common to both 'a politics of the "left"' and fascism. Second, so far as this relates to the left, its source is located not in the – complex (and dire) – social conditions and histories of the anti-capitalist revolutions of this century but – more simply – within Marxist doctrine as such: in the 'attempt to establish a definitive suture', 'a point of departure from which society can be *perfectly mastered and known*'.[112] Third, the evolution of Leninism into its authoritarian, that is, *Stalinist*, sequel is likewise put down to a theoretical source. How is that evolution to be accounted for? 'Quite simply [!], by the fact that the ontological privilege granted to the working class by Marxism was transferred from the social base to the political leadership of the mass movement.'[113] Old and well-known images of Marxism and Leninism: historical materialism, or just explanation, discarded, then, for what looks uncannily like common-or-garden anti-communism. Fourth, Laclau and Mouffe go so far as to conflate the whole of Marxism with its Stalinist, or authoritarian, forms by writing sometimes as though democracy was just *external* to it. They say at one point, for example: 'It is necessary to break with the view that democratic tasks are bonded to a bourgeois stage – only then will the obstacle preventing a permanent articulation between socialism and democracy be eliminated.'[114] The statement exploits a critical ambiguity in the expression 'democratic tasks', but let this pass. As if a whole Marxist tradition itself has not always rejected the view and the bond that the authors now deem it necessary to break with. This is, well and truly, the new-found virtue of the convert.

Fifth, finally, and by contrast with these prejudicial attitudes to Marxism, Laclau and Mouffe give us the warmest possible view of liberalism. 'It is not liberalism as such,' they aver, 'which should be called into question, for as an ethical principle which defends the liberty of the individual to fulfil his or her human capacities, it is more valid today than ever.'[115] Let us just accept, as par for the course here, the sudden appearance of 'human capacities'. I will even affirm a certain, *partial* agreement with the sentiment expressed, not being one of those Marxists for whom there is a total gulf between Marxism and liberalism, and no continuity of common values at all. But, in its overall context, the above accolade is a disgrace. Liberalism, not the suffering, squalor and misery of actual, liberal, capitalisms, but the fulfilment of human capacities. And one, Karl Marx: did he not also have something to say about the realization of the individual's human capacities?

If this is what the authors have taken with them from the school of Marxism, one can only wonder what the next stop on their itinerary might be.

Notes

1. Ernesto Laclau and Chantal Mouffe, *Hegemony and Socialist Strategy: Towards a Radical Democratic Politics* (hereafter HSS), Verso, London 1985, p. 4. Except where indicated otherwise, all emphasis in quotations is Laclau and Mouffe's.

2. Ellen Meiksins Wood, *The Retreat From Class*, Verso, London 1986, p. 47.

3. HSS, pp. 3–4.

4. See, e.g., HSS, pp. 30–31, 58, 67–8, 109, 174.

5. HSS, pp. 82–7.

6. HSS, pp. 156, 176–8, 192.

7. HSS, p. 177.

8. These expressions appear at HSS, pp. 21 (and 67), 4, 18, 88 (and 97), 69, 71, 70 (and 76), 76 (and 104), 76, 177, 68, 3, 100, 13–14, 55, 57 (and 61), 177, 177, 16, 68, 99. There is also, for good measure: 'classist categories', 'a monist perspective', 'dogmatic rationalism', 'class reductionism', 'a classist terrain', 'essentialist paradigms', 'essentialist assumption', 'essentialist solutions' – at pp. 11, 27, 34, 52 (and 85), 62, 77, 109, 134. And still the list is far from being complete.

9. HSS, p. 138.

10. HSS, p. 95.

11. HSS, p. 139.

12. HSS, p. 86. This echoes Althusser's well-known formula, 'From the first moment to the last, the lonely hour of the "last instance" never comes.' See Louis Althusser, *For Marx*, Verso, London 1969, p. 113.

13. See *For Marx*, pp. 101–4, 202–4; Louis Althusser and Étienne Balibar, *Reading Capital*, Verso, London 1970, pp. 93–7; and my 'Althusser's Marxism: An Account and Assessment', in Norman Geras, *Literature of Revolution*, Verso, London 1986, pp. 108 ff. For an excellent new assessment of Althusser's thought, see Gregory Elliott, *Althusser – The Detour of Theory*, Verso, London 1987.

14. HSS, pp. 87, 97.

15. HSS, pp. 144–5.

16. HSS, pp. 36, 3, 2.

17. HSS, pp. 2, 190, 192.

18. HSS, pp. 139–40. Emphasis added.

19. Ibid.

20. HSS, p. 13.

21. HSS, pp. 83–4. Emphasis added.

22. HSS, pp. 3, 7.

23. HSS, pp. 8–14.

24. HSS, pp. 19–21, 25.

25. HSS, pp. 25–7.

26. HSS, pp. 27–9.

27. HSS, pp. 29–36.

28. HSS, pp. 36–41.

29. HSS, pp. 48–54.
30. HSS, pp. 55–62, 65.
31. HSS, pp. 65–9.
32. HSS, pp. 97–9.
33. HSS, p. 4.
34. HSS, p. 22.
35. HSS, pp. 4, 18.
36. See text to note 25 above.
37. For Plekhanov, see HSS, pp. 23–4.
38. HSS, p. 69.
39. HSS, p. 97.
40. See *For Marx*, pp. 55–62.

41. See my *The Legacy of Rosa Luxemburg*, Verso, London 1976, pp. 111–31, especially pp. 120–21, 126–7.

42. For these five arguments, see 'The Mass Strike, the Political Party and the Trade Unions', in Mary-Alice Waters, ed., *Rosa Luxemburg Speaks*, New York 1970, respectively: (1) pp. 172, 176, 180–81, 199, 202–3; (2) p. 202; (3) pp. 192, 194, 196, 197–200; (4) pp. 165, 172, 176–8, 193, 196–7; (5) pp. 184–6.

43. For these eight points, see *Rosa Luxemburg Speaks*, respectively: (1) pp. 165, 166, 180; (2) pp. 166, 168; (3) pp. 170, 173; (4) p. 185; (5) pp. 177–8; (6) pp. 171–2, 185, 186–7; (7) pp. 170, 172, 179; (8) pp. 173–6.

44. HSS, pp. 10–11.

45. Cf. Althusser: 'this method which is constantly *judging* cannot *make the slightest judgement of any totality unlike itself*. Could there be a franker admission that it *merely judges itself, recognizes itself behind the objects it considers* ...' *For Marx*, p. 60.

46. HSS, pp. 12–13.

47. A last 'detail' here. The authors write: 'Recently, a number of studies have discussed the fatalist or non-fatalist character of Luxemburgist spontaneism. In our opinion, however, these have given excessive emphasis to a relatively secondary problem, such as the alternative between mechanical collapse and conscious intervention of the class. The assertion that capitalism will mechanically collapse is so absurd that, as far as we know, nobody, has upheld it.' As the only one amongst this 'number of studies' they actually cite is my own, I may be permitted to observe that the section of it to which they refer sought to show, with full textual documentation and a clarity, if I may say so, which leaves no room for misunderstanding, that Rosa Luxemburg upheld the thesis that 'capitalism will mechanically collapse'; but why, *despite that*, she believed 'conscious intervention of the class' still to be necessary, since capitalist collapse would otherwise issue in barbarism. My arguments and interpretation of her texts might, of course, have been wrong. But it is indicative of Laclau and Mouffe's happy-go-lucky way with ideas that, without bothering to show that or how they were, they just *assert*, against them, that her 'statements concerning the inevitability of socialism are not simply concessions to the rhetoric of the time or the result of a psychological need ... but rather the nodal point giving meaning to her entire theoretical and strategic structure.' HSS, pp. 42–3 n. 8.

48. See text to note 30 above.

49. HSS, pp. 52–3.

50. See 'On the Special Features of Russia's Historical Development', in Leon Trotsky, *1905*, London 1972, pp. 333, 338, 343–4. Readers may enjoy checking for themselves what I mean by 'cheek by jowl' here.

51. See Leon Trotsky, *The Permanent Revolution and Results and Prospects*, London 1962, pp. 169–77; and *1905*, pp. 3–11.

52. See text to note 18 above.

53. HSS, pp. 30, 41.

54. HSS, p. 71. Emphasis added.

55. Ibid.

56. HSS, pp. 107, 108. The second emphasis in (ii) is mine.

57. HSS, p. 108.

58. Lenin in 'Materialism and Empirio-Criticism', *Collected Works*, Moscow 1960–1970, vol. 14, p. 344.

59. HSS, p. 110. And cf. the characteristically blunt opinion of the same Marxist 'essentialist', concerning 'the stupid claim to have "risen above" materialism and idealism, to have transcended this "obsolete" antithesis ...', Lenin, *Collected Works*, vol. 14, p. 341.

60. HSS, p. 105.

61. HSS, p. 93; and cf. p. 134.

62. HSS, pp. 134, 142.

63. HSS, p. 135. My emphasis.

64. HSS, p. 115.

65. HSS, p. 138.

66. HSS, pp. 86–7.

67. HSS, pp. 112, 139; and cf. p. 142.

68. HSS, pp. 140, 136–8.

69. See text to note 64 above. The argument cited there is of this form: 'Horses cannot, therefore, be the origin of stampedes of horses – not even in the limited sense of being endowed with powers that render galloping possible – as all "galloping" depends on precise geographical conditions of possibility.' I criticize arguments of this general type, which by sleight-of-hand discount or minimize the role of 'subjects' and their powers, in Chapter IV of *Marx and Human Nature: Refutation of a Legend*, Verso, London 1983 – see, especially, pp. 106–8, 111–16.

70. See André Glucksmann, 'A Ventriloquist Structuralism', in *New Left Review*, eds., *Western Marxism – A Critical Reader*, Verso, London 1977, p. 285.

71. HSS, p. 177.

72. HSS, pp. 116, 96.

73. HSS, p. 58.

74. HSS, pp. 86–7.

75. See text to note 10 above.

76. HSS, pp. 99, 111, 114, 122 (and 130 and 136).

77. HSS, pp. 110, 93.

78. HSS, pp. 107, 110–11; and cf. pp. 106–7, 113, 134.

79. For what explication there is, and other appearances, of 'regularity in dispersion', see HSS, pp. 105–6, 135, 136, 142.

80. HSS, pp. 85, 104. My emphasis.

81. HSS, pp. 111–12.

82. HSS, pp. 110–11; and cf. pp. 135, 142.

83. HSS, pp. 111, 114 (and 142).

84. HSS, pp. 112, 129.

85. HSS, pp. 86, 193.

86. HSS, pp. 167, 170–71.

87. See text to note 77 above.

88. HSS, p. 65.

89. HSS, pp. 86, 190.

90. HSS (in turn), pp. 133, 137, 136, 66, 131, 160, 161.

91. HSS, p. 4.

92. See text to note 27 above.

93. HSS, pp. 86, 87, 168; and pp. 5, 169, 174.

94. HSS, pp. 152–3, 116–17 (and 181, 188). On this, see *Marx and Human Nature*, pp. 96–7.

95. HSS, pp. 28, 174–5. Is this particular '-ism' meant to join those of racism and sexism, so making up a noxious trinity? If so, one ought to note the asymmetry involved in that extension. Racists claim the superiority of their 'race', and sexists claim or just live by the domination of men. 'Classists', in Laclau and Mouffe's usage, are not those who defend the power and privilege of a dominant class but, on the contrary, those who oppose this class from the standpoint of the class it exploits – thereby turning the latter, apparently, into a 'privileged subject'.

96. HSS, p. 3; and cf. what is said about natural rights, p. 184.

97. HSS, pp. 153–4.

98. HSS, p. 125.

99. HSS, p. 154.

100. See HSS, p. 131.

101. HSS, p. 158. Emphasis added.

102. HSS, p. 41.

103. See *The Retreat from Class*, pp. 64–70.

104. HSS, pp. 1, 3, 4, 166, 176 (and 152, 167, 189, 191).

105. HSS, p. 185.

106. See, e.g., HSS, p. 159.

107. HSS, p. 156.

108. See HSS, pp. 152–66.

109. HSS, pp. 1–2, 87.

110. See my 'The Controversy About Marx and Justice', in *Literature of Revolution*, particularly pp. 42–3 – or *New Left Review* 150, March/April 1985, pp. 75–6.

111. HSS, pp. 84–5, 87, 120.

112. HSS, pp. 187–8. Emphasis added.

113. HSS, p. 56; and cf. p. 59.

114. HSS, p. 58; and see also what is said about the 'communist militant' at p. 55 and about 'democratic rights and freedoms' at pp. 61–2.

115. HSS, p. 184.

Ex-Marxism Without Substance:
A Rejoinder

There is a discursive strategy commonly adopted by politicians, particularly at election time, in the face of discomforting questions. It consists of appearing to respond to a questioner but without actually answering her question. The thing has the external form of an answer but is not one. Practically everyone knows how this works. The politician subtly alters the terms of the question to suit his own convenience, or substitutes a different one, or just repeats what he has already said (which may have prompted the question in the first place), or talks about something else altogether – or uses some combination of these moves. In any case, he does not answer. It is with just such a 'politician's reply' that Ernesto Laclau and Chantal Mouffe have responded to my criticisms of their book. To have expected that they would receive these with any warmth would obviously have been foolish. But no even moderately careful reader, such as one might think each of them had good enough reason in this case to be, can have been left in doubt as to what the criticisms were. I lay them out in summary and then show, one by one, how Laclau and Mouffe have thought fit to deal with them.

After a brief introduction, to whose subject matter I shall later return, my critique of *Hegemony and Socialist Strategy* falls into two main sections. In the first, I argue that the book presents an impoverishing caricature of the Marxist tradition, and in the second, that what it offers instead is intellectually empty. As each of these arguments itself falls into two major parts, there are four contentions here: (1) that the authors caricature Marxism by their habitual procedure of confronting it with spurious, absurdly rigid antitheses; (2) that the account they render of some key Marxist thinkers is a travesty of the tradition, reducing and devaluing it and distorting many of its ideas; (3) that their own social theory is all but vacuous: conceptually slippery at decisive points and unable to explain anything specific; and (4) that it is also normatively indeterminate, fit to support virtually any kind of politics, progressive or reactionary. In addition, early in the first of the essay's two sections I introduce a theme which is then pursued as and where relevant through both of them, namely: (5) that in the book's inflated rhetoric of 'essentialism', 'suture', 'closure', there is a facile criticism of the thought of others, undisciplined by responsible criteria and amounting to a form of obscurantism. Finally, in a concluding section on the authors' overt politics, I note (6) how disappointingly thin are the ideas on democracy from two wouldbe 'radical' democrats and, worse than thin, the appearance here also of some of the more standard tropes of Cold War anti-Marxism. Half a dozen central arguments, then.

1. Polarities

Laclau and Mouffe begin their response to the first one by misstating it. I am supposed to have reproached them with having '*based [their] main theoretical conclusions*' on rigid oppositions; with having 'counterposed two polar and exclusive alternatives, without considering the possibility of intermediate solutions that avoid both extremes'.[1] Not so. And indeed the opposite of the point I make repeatedly: which is that they *criticize Marxism* in the light of excessively polarized alternatives, whilst allowing themselves the intermediacy they need and, more, downright imprecision and evasiveness. This contrast is formulated – explicitly – at least three times and is fundamental to the structure of my critique.[2] The misstatement is an enabling one, in the sense of helping to yield the appearance of answers where there are none, via a shift from the polarity criticized to some other.

(i) Take first, for the unadorned purity of the displacement, the third of the examples I discussed, objective interests. As Laclau and Mouffe do not trouble to remind *New Left Review*'s readers which particular antithesis it was I took exception to in this matter, let me do it. It was the 'clear' 'alternative' (their words): either one has a theory in which 'an absolutely united working class will become transparent to itself at the moment of proletarian chiliasm' in which case one can believe in objective interests; or one abandons that theory, and the notion is then 'meaningless'. I pointed out that a concept of objective interests does not require belief in all of *that*. No Marxist has to choose between objective interests with chiliasm and the rest and rejecting the concept altogether. To which the 'reply' now is: we do not criticize the notion of interests as such, only that of objective interests (as though I had said different); and because we know there are interests, it is not a rigid 'either/or' alternative we put forward – meaning presumably that interests as Laclau and Mouffe conceive them stand between objective interests and just no interests. But *this* was not the alternative I criticized and *their own* conception of these things, however 'intermediate', is not pertinent to what I did criticize: namely, the ludicrous choice they posed for Marxists. Such is what they call showing 'in all three cases' how *my* criticism is based on 'misrepresentation'.[3]

It might have been more charitable to pass over this as just the authors' way of retreating from a formulation they did not wish to defend, were it not for the fact that they have simply replaced that one with others of its kind: to wit, that the idea of objective interests presupposes something inscribed in the nature of agents 'as a gift from Heaven'; and that 'only God and Geras know' how this is compatible with a 'non-essentialist' social theory.

Well, really... I had already noted an occurrence of this gift-from-Heaven 'thesis' as a substitute for serious argument, over the question of human nature.[4] To no avail. Not just my own and others' defence of the latter concept on carefully reasoned, theoretical and empirical, grounds but a whole literature on human needs seems to have passed these humanists by. Apostles of intellectual openness and pluralism, they can see no creditable basis for a view here different from theirs; it could only be a slightly crazed conception of socialist revolution or, if not that, then – this. Mark, as relevant to another issue I shall come to, their use of the language of religious faith – 'chiliasm', 'gift from Heaven', 'God' – as a negative reference point.

(ii) On the question of relative autonomy things are slightly more complex. Laclau and Mouffe are willing this time to defend the rigid alternative I criticized them for posing, so demonstrating that I did not misrepresent them; but only in conjunction with pursuing the claim that I did misrepresent them. No problem: they simply obfuscate the contours of the *particular* antithesis I complained of – as addressed by them to Marxists – in order to show again how they, for their part, steer a most judicious course between extremes. Citing a passage from their book which, this too, they forbear now to put before the reader, I gave evidence of the choice they defined *for Marxism*: either so strong a notion of determination that the concept of relative autonomy becomes 'redundant'; or else the entities theorized as relatively autonomous are simply 'not determined' by the set of basic determinants, which cannot therefore be that. This is a choice in effect, I argued, between these determinants determining totally and not determining at all, 'explaining everything and determining nothing'; a choice, for Marxists, of either openly embracing economism or kissing historical materialism goodbye. At the same time, I made it perfectly clear, not once and not twice but three times at *that* point in my text, what the authors saw as the proper solution of this Marxist 'dilemma': namely (and quoting them), 'plurality of political and social spaces'; and again 'irreducible plurality of the social'; and once more (in my own voice) 'plurality'. Not only that, but I went on later, apropos of 'hegemonic articulation', to give an account of this plurality – complex and fluid; 'crisscrossed by antagonisms'; with no privileged centre but many articulatory practices; of multiply constituted, mutually limiting identities, struggles, movements; and so forth – an account that could have left no one in ignorance of the fact that Laclau and Mouffe do believe in the reciprocal effectivity or mutual interaction of one thing and another.[5]

In response I told a simple story. If I am chained to a post by the ankle, then the chain is a basic determinant of my lifestyle since it will powerfully affect it – *and* I enjoy a relative autonomy in what I can do. The story had one point and one point only. This was not to suggest that, say, capitalist relations of production are to the bourgeois state *exactly like* a chain is to a person chained. Nor was it to deny that there is room for serious argument and difference in this difficult area: I expressed myself – again, quite explicitly – to the contrary, my theme being precisely that it was the way this question, amongst others, was posed in *Hegemony and Socialist Strategy* that foreclosed the possibility of any fruitful intellectual engagement with a flat, arbitrary 'either/or'. No, the point of the story was to show that a fundamental determinant, to be one, need not explain or determine everything; that Marxists are not bound to choose – in plainest words – 'between the most extravagant economic reductionism and what the authors here commend to us, just plurality' (or between the alternatives, as I also put it, 'Either one is all or all are one'); that we could just hold, about the state in capitalist society, 'that capitalist relations of production, and the configuration of classes they define, are *primary* to the explanation of such polities'.[6]

A Relation of Omnipotence

There are three components to Laclau and Mouffe's effort of reply.[7] First, they present my argument in a form that leaves it nicely ambiguous what I was criticizing: whether – and as I was – the all-determining/not-determining alternative they lay down for Marxism, thereby rendering relative autonomy unthinkable in historical-materialist terms; or their rejection of this concept themselves owing to the overly rigid constraints on their own thought – as I was not. This confected ambiguity then allows them carefully to explain, over and again, that *they*, you see, *do* recognize 'the relative efficacy of each sphere', and do *not* 'set up a rigid alternative between total autonomy and absolute subordination'. Another evasion. A displacement of my question, which remains without a reply, as we shall see.

Second, they charge me with 'sleight of hand' and a 'trick', because with the example of the chain I transform a relation of determination into a relation of mere limitation. The short answer to this is that I do not. But Laclau and Mouffe simply *leave out* anything inconvenient for them. For all its artificiality, the example was put together with the degree of care necessary to my purpose, which was to give a model of powerful but less than total determination, combining both limits and pressures. After describing how it might limit me, I therefore wrote, 'The chain *not only limits* me, negatively; it *also compels* me to certain actions'; and illustrated this point in turn.[8] So important to the authors is it that determination is not mere limitation that they repeat it three times in a dozen lines. How was it possible, then, for them to overlook just this aspect of the argument, and in dealing out a language of trickery at that? I do not know. But a worrying pattern is becoming clear here. It is for all the world as if they were investing everything on the circumstance that their readers will not simultaneously be reading my essay: a rather short-sighted approach to intellectual debate.

Third, and exposing the futility of all this, Laclau and Mouffe just repeat the concept of determination I had put in question. Determination, it so 'happens', is not only not mere limitation, it is not any combination of limits and pressures (or conditions, influences, causes, etc.) short of the whole works. Thus, we are told: 'the base/superstructure model affirms that the base ... *determines* the superstructure, in the same way that the movements of a hand determine the movements of its shadow on a wall';

and that this is a relation of *expression*; and that the concepts of determination in the last instance and relative autonomy are '*logically* incompatible'; and that the former of them denotes 'a relation of omnipotence'. Attempts to complicate the model with a notion of 'mediations' do not change anything, since entities related via mediations are, strictly, not even separate. There can be no effectively autonomous entities if determination in the last instance is 'an *a priori* truth', because that is then part of the essence of such entities. I think it will be readily agreed that these observations do restate the view of determination I criticized. But what is the argument for it? There is no argument. That is what determination *means*. We have been given a series of stipulative definitions, nothing more. The authors themselves obscurely appreciate the point when, after nearly a thousand words of this, they confess parenthetically – about one of their stipulations, but it applies to the whole lot – that all their 'reasoning' here is 'actually, unnecessary' since affirming fundamental determination and effective autonomy simultaneously 'was inconsistent from the beginning'. That was, indeed, what I cited them as holding, and then contested (as being the 'merest verbal edict').[9] How is it an answer, though, simply to say it again, even several times? It is confirmation of the criticism and not a reply to it. Further, if this is the level of the discussion, I can just open my dictionary, where the *first* meanings given for 'determine' are 'to put terms or bounds to' and 'to limit'.[10] From 'anti-essentialist' theoreticians of discursive multiformity – and who invoke the authority of Wittgenstein to boot – one could have expected a little better.

For, to imagine that the history of Marxist thought could be so adjudicated by definitional fiat is preposterous. Starting with Marx's *1859 Preface, fons et origo* in this matter, the relationship under discussion is formulated not in one univocal definition but with a series of terms, of different force ('corresponds', 'conditions', 'determines'), and even there only 'as the *guiding thread* of my studies'.[11] The subsequent history of Marxism could be written as one long meditation, with real differences internal to it, on the exact nature, scope, strength, of that relationship. But an *omnipotent* base and a superstructure determined *like a shadow on the wall*: that is the reductionist caricature I made objection to, repeated in spades. If there have been Marxisms like it, other Marxisms refused so to be, and the fault of Laclau and Mouffe's whole standpoint, as I showed, is to rule such refusal incoherent, within any historical materialism meaningfully so called, by simple diktat: with determination, sorry, no relative autonomy! One (relevant) episode of recent intellectual history is now cast in a new light. All of Althusser's project appears to have been based on a semantic mistake, since he insisted, as no one more vehemently, that relations of determination are not relations of expression, when... they are.

Systems of Domination

Setting word-play aside, therefore, I just put again the question Laclau and Mouffe have not looked squarely in the face. Why is there no logical space between 'the most extravagant economic reductionism' and mere 'plurality'? Why no space for a notion of explanatory *primacy*? How *could* this be ruled out as a matter of logic alone? Let us take only one argument that has been important within Marxism. This is the argument that it makes a difference whether or not the political institutions of a capitalist society are parliamentary-democratic ones resting on an ensemble of 'liberal' rights, practices and procedures: a 'quite enormous difference', as Trotsky put it in connection with Nazism, and for workers' organizations, 'a question of political life or death'. The point has been formulated in various ways. As by Trotsky himself, who spoke of parliamentary democracy and fascism as two 'different systems of (class) domination', within the former of which the workers are able to create 'elements of proletarian democracy'; 'defensive bulwarks'; 'within the bourgeois democracy, by utilizing it, by fighting against it, their own strongholds and bases of *proletarian democracy*: the trade unions, the political parties, the educational and sport clubs, the cooperatives, etc.' Or as by Luxemburg, whose ideas on parliamentary democracy I have myself criticized in

another respect, but for whom it was 'one of the most powerful
and indispensable means of carrying on the class struggle', 'necessary to the working class because it creates the political forms
(autonomous administration, electoral rights, etc.) which will serve
... as fulcrums in its task of transforming bourgeois society'.[12]
However formulated, it is a view that has been common to all
serious Marxist thinkers, and it has no credible sense other than
that political institutions and structures have a specific effectivity
of their own and are therefore *not* the mere epiphenomena ('sha-
dows') of class or economic power. And – contrary to the 'simplistic' view the authors here allege – political democracy is not
reducible to this: it is *not* the pure expression, or simple instrument,
of the interests of a dominant class. As a *reality* with important
consequences, as (to some degree) a separate and independent
institutional configuration, its structures and procedures must be
given due causal weight.

At the same time, the Marxist tradition has never accepted
the view of the state propagated by liberalism and pluralist political
science: as a sort of neutral arena; or arbiter or mediator between
and 'above' classes. Marxists reject such notions because, in their
judgement, the competing influence, the limits *and* the pressures,
exerted by structures of exploitation and class carry a *greater* causal
weight, and their effect is that the state tends to give capitalist
interests priority over those of working people – not in everything
and without exception, but in general, most of the time, in what
matters most. Hence, *relative* autonomy only; but it is no less real
for that and does not mean state forms are merely nugatory: Marxists are also capable of thinking in terms of more and less. Nor
is the judgement they make here, concerning the explanatory
primacy of relations of production and class, 'an *a priori* truth': it
is an empirical hypothesis, albeit of long historical range; subject
to exceptions as well as to confirmation; subject also, in principle,
to the possibility of being falsified should there (turn out to) be
too much and too cogent historical counter-evidence to it. The
serious and interesting issues at stake, therefore, are not advanced
a single millimetre by bandying about definitions of a thought-

stifling kind ('determines' is 'omnipotent', 'mediations' means 'not separate', and so forth). What the mechanisms of bourgeois hegemony are, what the exact ways in which class power determines – effects, limits or conditions – political results at the level of the state, is one such issue. How much explanatory importance is to be assigned to: (a) the modes of *economic power* as such, the various ways in which capitalist interests and actions either indirectly constrain or bring direct pressure to bear upon the state; (b) factors of *social composition*, that is, the extent to which the class origins and background of those who make, administer and adjudicate law, align them with the dominant economic class; (c) factors of *structural limitation*, in other words, the (differential) degrees to which different types of state and their constituent structures – historically shaped as in every case they have been by some particular nexus of dominant class interests – block or hinder access to decision making by the majority of the ruled?

These are difficult questions, in which the assessment of evidence is critical. More than one view about them is possible, obviously. A lot of Marxists make the sort of judgement they do in this matter because they consider the volume of evidence in favour of the historical-materialist hypothesis to be rather formidable. One can perfectly well respect other, competing views, other assessments, of the historical evidence, soberly presented and conscientiously argued for. More: any serious Marxism is duty bound to engage with these. What is much harder, however, is to respect a view, from people themselves quite lately Marxist, in which any rational form of Marxism has all at once become *unthinkable*, and by act of definition. This smacks of something else: intemperate flight, perhaps, or mentality of repentance; in any case, what can aptly be called intellectual 'closure'.[13]

Double Logic

(iii) The other of the extreme antitheses I objected to concerned the process of unification of a fragmentary working class. It was Laclau and Mouffe's alternative – formulated in connection with

Luxemburg's thought – either 'necessary laws', 'proletarianization', 'crisis' (unification, that is, by sheer economic determinism), or else fragmentation is 'permanent' (and class, consequently, not fundamental to the unities which politics constructs). My reply to this, as before, was '*tertium datur*': a common class situation and some economic tendencies of capitalism could be seen, not as inexorably producing proletarian unity, just as providing the conditional basis for a socialist politics with that goal.[14] The authors now complain of a 'flagrant' misquotation on my part. I omitted to say that they were here only engaging in a 'game' of 'frontiers', wherein they extended in turn the 'operative area' covered by the different logics of structural determinism and spontaneism. The above alternative *only* arises from a sort of experimental *reductio ad absurdum*, in which Marxism is taken in its most 'essentialist', 'exclusively determinist' versions. But, outside of that. . . well, they themselves not only 'pointed out the presence of a double historical logic in the text of Rosa Luxemburg' – determinism *and* spontaneism – they 'presented the history of Marxism ... as a sustained effort to escape the "either/or" logic of determinism'.[15]

Were it not for a rather special feature of it, one would have to think this argument had been concocted for a joke. But as it carries with it the accusation that I am intellectually 'dishonest', or, at least, *maybe* dishonest, I assume more serious intent. Let us, therefore, talk a little further about relations of 'expression'. It can sometimes happen that in a single phrase or gesture you suddenly see summed up – 'expressed' – the whole outlook or disposition or character of a person. Just so, in one paragraph here there is captured, concentrated, the seemingly limitless arbitrariness of what has now become of the thought of Laclau and Mouffe. The two of them, unconstrained not only by what others but even by what they themselves write, discreetly refrain from mentioning that what their 'reply' terms the 'double historical logic' in Luxemburg's thought was also called, in their book, an 'irreducible dualism' and 'a double void'. How could they possibly have forgotten this when, as I think they will acknowledge, my critique did rather focus on that last phrase?[16] And they tactfully decline here to say that what is now characterized as Marxism's 'sustained effort etc.' goes under the rubric, in the book – on page after page – of 'dualism', 'spurious dualism', 'the dualism of classical Marxism', 'exactly the same dualism'. And why does it? Because, according to them, the two logics, the two sides of the said dualism, are inconsistent with one another: not 'two positive and different explanatory principles' (as they put it apropos Luxemburg), but 'ultimately incoherent' (apropos Gramsci).[17] True, they do not establish, they merely assert, this inconsistency, in the very manner we have just witnessed again with 'determines' and relative autonomy. Still, that is what they do assert, time and time again, and so the 'game' of frontiers is really *it* and that is why I took it to be it. It is *their* contention, not mine, that a historical-materialist framework excludes any *coherent* use by its proponents of (good) concepts like relative autonomy, hegemony, overdetermination, Luxemburgist 'spontaneity', and so on; *their* contention that it is an ineradicably 'essentialist', 'economist', 'reductionist' framework. For any logical mind persuaded by this contention and not confused by the momentary exigency of having to find *something* to say, that imposes a choice between straight, unmitigated economic determinism and whatever is thought to be the separate and opposed logic of the aforesaid (good) concepts. But this is exactly the alternative disclosed by the so-called game of frontiers. And this is precisely the reason Laclau and Mouffe have taken the 'post-Marxist' path. And then, when it is pointed out that it is a falsely polarized alternative, reposing on a caricature of historical materialism, they turn round in all injured innocence and say in effect, *by way of vindication*: but this was 'only' a caricature – a '*reductio ad absurdum*' – of Marxism, which we *knew* and we *said* to be more complex actually, embodying other, better logics *as well*. They 'only' neglect to observe that it is a complexity they have condemned as incoherent: void. Void, yes indeed – right word, wrong object – and bottomless.

The character of response, then, is becoming all too plain. To the first criticism made of their book the best these writers have to offer is blank repetition of the point contested; and apart from

that there is just evasion or displacement of the questions actually
raised, strategic exclusion of key aspects, now of my argument,
now of their own, denial of having posed a choice they manifestly
have posed; and then some bluster ('God and Geras') and a touch
of personal accusation. It will get no better. But already there
is material enough and more that I could, were I so minded,
level a charge of intellectual dishonesty of my own. I do not.
Partly because I believe it to be rare – people generally deceiving
themselves before 'deceiving' others – and partly because when
it happens, as I suppose it sometimes does, it is impossible without
close personal knowledge to know that it has. There is, in any
case, a more plausible explanation for all this – to which point
I will return. For now, let it suffice to say that, whatever the
explanation for it, one thing is crystal clear: it is the *form* of 'making
a reply' that is everything here, the quality or substance of it
– nothing. To adapt a well-known aphorism concerning justice:
a reply need not actually be made, but it must be seen to be
made.

2. Marxists

Hegemony and Socialist Strategy unfolds a view of various Marxist
thinkers which, my essay argued, is systematically impoverishing,
a travesty. Two items preface what there is of a response to that
argument.[18] The first item is a summary redescription of the authors' project as they see it; but in the same artless spirit we just
now encountered: their book sought to show that 'Marxist thought'
has 'been a persistent effort . . . to distance itself from essentialism',
the emergence 'internal to Marxism itself' of other, better logics.
That is what their book sought to show. Not that Marxism *is*
the 'essentialism' (principal, omnipresent, Laclau-Mouffian epithet
of its deficiency), is the 'reductionism', 'economism' and the rest;
and that *every* Marxist effort to 'distance itself' has therefore yielded
for its author a dualism, whether 'irreducible' or 'spurious' or
'incoherent'. No, the 'persistent effort' and 'internal' to Marxism.

We can leave behind this species of self-presentation. We have already seen its secret: suddenly and conveniently ascribing *to Marxism* what is everywhere else claimed to be logically *incompatible* with it *qua* 'essentialism' etc. My own critique, if I may say so, expressed the whole matter rather more clearly. At the very beginning of the argument that Laclau and Mouffe had produced a travesty, I wrote, 'To be absolutely precise about this: it is not that they deny all the strengths, insights, contributions of theoretical value, as they construe them, to be found in the work of Marxist *writers....* But such elements of value are all stipulated as being *external* to the real parameters of Marxism.'[19] If this characterization is inaccurate, we are owed a reason why it is now necessary to be on a 'post-Marxist' terrain at all; why, to put the same thing differently, these various 'elements of value' in the work of Marxist writers do not show (what they do show) that not all Marxism has been 'essentialist' and reductionist; why, to turn their own equivocation right round upon the authors, Marxist thought has not indeed contained – 'internal' to it – the '*anti*-essentialism' they here briefly allow that it has; why *Marxism*, then, is not made rich and current again through having so restored to it that inner wealth of which it was earlier stripped. The entire 'post-Marxist' standpoint will begin helplessly to unravel.

The second item, complementing this positive self-image, is an image of another stripe. Laclau and Mouffe express themselves amazed by my view 'that Bernstein and Sorel "abandoned" Marxism', adding: 'and in Geras this has the unmistakable connotation of betrayal.' In fact, 'abandoned' is their word and not mine, but no matter, I do say that Bernstein and Sorel rejected, or broke with, Marxism (just as the authors have now done).[20] There could, I suppose, be room for argument to the contrary about this. It would be interesting to see some. But, in any event, it is not a wildly eccentric view. In Bernstein's case, at least, it is the view of Peter Gay, Carl Schorske and George Lichtheim amongst other scholars of a notably different political outlook from mine. It is also, I submit, entailed by what Laclau and Mouffe themselves aver concerning both Bernstein and Sorel.[21] But what about 'betrayal'? The rude fact is that I say nothing whatsoever about either Bernstein or Sorel having betrayed anything. Hence: 'unmistakable connotation of'. So introduced, 'betrayal' quickly *displaces* 'abandonment'. The authors wax indignant: 'What can we think about this ridiculous story of "betrayal" and "abandonment"? What would one make of a history of philosophy which claimed that Aristotle betrayed Plato ... that Marx betrayed Hegel?' They tell us. 'We' would think that for the person who approaches things in this way 'the betrayed doctrine is an object of *worship* ... a religious object' (mark it again, the pejorative reference to religious belief). Further... 'We know the story very well: Bernstein betrayed Marx; European social-democracy betrayed the working class; the Soviet bureaucracy betrayed the revolution ... thus, the only trustees of "Revolution" and "Science" are the small sects belonging to imaginary Internationals which ... are permanently splitting.' I think Laclau and Mouffe may here be wanting to suggest to the reader that Geras is some kind of a Trotskyist and 'we' all know about them. It is desperate stuff.

If it is true that I am a worshipper of Marxism or relevant that I am some kind of a Trotskyist, one should be able to show how this is reflected in, and vitiates, *specific* criticisms and arguments that I *in fact* direct at their book. Better still, as the product of a devout, unquestioning mind and vitiated, these criticisms and arguments should be no trouble to deal with: one could, then, just reply to (as in: answer) one or two of them, instead of throwing up one smokescreen after another. I mean, what, otherwise, are we to think? What I, personally, do think, is that this is testimony again to the meaning of discursive 'openness' and 'pluralism'. The most (let us just say) frontal criticism of Marxism and all its works – that is good, plain creative intellectual endeavour. But defence of Marxism, against this same criticism and because it is judged to be (let us just say) uncompelling, *this* can only be sectarianism and piety. Another very well-known story: non-Marxists can, but Marxists never do, adopt their opinions and judgements on a reflective, questioning, considered basis. It confirms – in a different register, so to say – the justness of the charge of travesty. For, closure and chiliasm, fixity and reduction, 'essentialism' *ad nauseam* and more of the same: how *could* Marxism now be entertained by a thoughtful, open intellect, be defended any other way than piously?

As for 'betrayal': although it has been overused, I believe this notion *is* sometimes apt, in political as in personal affairs. People can betray comrades or supporters; or their own stated principles. I think an excellent example of the latter case to be, precisely, the conduct of many 'anti-militarist' social-democratic leaders at the outbreak of the First World War. But in intellectual matters, in the assessment of theoretical approaches or paradigms – their strengths, their problems and their failures – the question of betrayal is neither here nor there. Betrayal of a *theory*, a conception of history or society, this is indeed a nonsense; and so it would be to think that Bernstein or anybody else had 'betrayed Marx' – or Marx*ism*. I do not. What has possibly confused these writers is a view of *themselves* imputed to me on the basis that my tone of address was a sharp rather than warm, congenial one. Difficult as it may be for them to accept these, there are other reasons for that than the break with Marxism as such. *Ex*-Marxist opinion and criticism, also, can be such as to command the respect of Marxists. Where it is of a measured and serious kind, they have a responsibility to try to meet it in like spirit. More: it may have to be acknowledged as identifying some weakness(es) within Marxist thought in need of being made good, since there are enough of those.[22] (But *which* social theory lacks them?) By the same token, however, there is no obligation on Marxists to be impressed by any old collection of facile exaggerations and stale anti-Marxist prejudices. That is – once again – harder to respect, and so is the relentless diminishing of a vital intellectual tradition into a shrunken, parodied remnant of itself: harder to respect, coming from anyone; hardest, coming from people who *might* have been expected to know better. If any concept of betrayal applies here, it is only betrayal of the intellectual standards proper to serious enquiry and debate. Laclau and Mouffe may not be able to agree with these, my reasons, much less find them welcome, but that's the way it goes. One puts one's work in the public domain and then sees.

The Stigma of 'Essentialism'

From the friendly self-description and the indignation the authors proceed to what they style a 'point by point' reply to my main criticisms of their treatment of Marxist thought. Their first – which purports to respond to my first – point here is that I have accused them of 'choosing *at random* a group of Marxist thinkers' (my emphasis), and this they have not done, for they were narrating an intellectual *history*. They certainly make life easy for themselves. I gave a detailed account of the intellectual history they narrated, displaying how, for every Marxist thinker there treated, effectively *the same thing* had been construed: namely, some (smaller or greater) amount of headway, against the thinker's Marxist economism and 'essentialism', towards understanding the world (in terms of con-tingency and what have you); but always failure ultimately to leave the said deficiencies behind, and hence a dualism. Finding the standards of demonstration deployed unimpressive, I commented, with satiric but not at all frivolous intent, that it was a simple game; in which 'You take some Marxist, any Marxist will do...' and then go through the one reductive exegetical routine. My point was not that the authors *had chosen* Marxists haphazardly. A line which runs from Luxemburg and Kautsky through Plekha-nov, Labriola, the Austro-Marxists, Lenin, Trotsky, Gramsci, Althusser – that is not just any random bunch of Marxists (which is why I spoke, in introducing my summary of this, of 'the treatment meted out here seriatim to a number of Marxism's more important thinkers'). My point was that, with the intellectual methods in question, it makes no difference, *whichever Marxist thinker you choose* you can effortlessly 'show' the same thing.[23]

I *then* went on to identify the reason for this. We are afforded no demonstration by Laclau and Mouffe of how, in the writers treated, Marxist categories have been inflated into 'essences'; thus no demonstration that these actually are 'essentialist'. Bare use of the categories is proof, *ipso facto*, of 'essentialism'. To be the latter's victim – or perpetrator – it suffices that you be a Marxist, irrespective of whether or not you reduce everything to class or economic, or any other singular, significance. For, 'essentialism' functions doubly in the discourse of *Hegemony and Socialist Strategy*: as concept and as stigma – and these two are, so to put it, dislocated. As concept, it is roughly given by the notion of 'expressive totality'. It is monism, reduction of apparent complexity to the underlying simplicity of an essence, explanation of the whole by reference to one part, and so on. As stigma, however, 'essentialism' is compatible with *not* explaining everything by reduction to one essence. It is merely some categorial discrimination, within social 'plurality', between more and less important. As I pointed out, the authors not only do *not* show that for their chosen Marxists class, say, *was* all-explanatory, they *do* show that it was *not* all-explanatory (the basis, this, for 'essentialism's' companion stigma, 'dualism'). That does not deter them in the slightest from the charge of 'essentialism': a sort of littler 'essentialism' in which everything is explained by the one essence, except for what isn't. It is a bit like some mediaeval tests for witchcraft.

But to this whole argument Laclau and Mouffe have nothing to say, a rather curious silence in a 'point by point' reply. The fact is – and as I argued next – they themselves involuntarily show (but now as in: display) the genuine meaning of essentialism: promotion of a concept or schema to the point where it is just omnipresent in the real, despite every evidence to the contrary. Such is their own account of Marxism, history or no; a self-enclosed, unfalsifiable theoretical matrix.[24]

Their second point, then – which responds to my fourth – is this: 'we are supposed to have contradicted ourselves by saying that Marxism is monist and dualist at the same time. But there is no contradiction here: what we asserted is that Marxism becomes dualist as a result of the failure of monism. A theory that starts by being pluralist would run no risk of becoming dualist.' That is the whole thing, undiminished, from beginning to end. At least this time Laclau and Mouffe have come up with an original sort

of response to criticism: not just a repetition of the position criticized, but a repetition, as near as makes no difference, *of the critic
himself*. As any reader can verify with but a moment's effort, what
is proffered here as a reply virtually paraphrases a section of my
criticism, the questioned being simply given back as the answer.
I myself set out this logic of theirs: that *because* it was monist whilst
the world was not, Marxism has had to be dualist in order to
cope.[25] But this, which they take as a finishing, is only the starting
line for any half-way serious reply. For, I went on to argue that
it is a perverse logic. It rests on merely *ruling* Marxism to be always-
already monist, in every one of its guises and lineages; and then,
by the process of impoverishment I protested against, discounting
all conceptual matter testifying otherwise – the likes of 'spontaneity', political initiative, hegemony, relative autonomy – as foreign
to its nature, and so the other half of a dualism. The question
which my critique clearly posed is: but what, then, leaving aside
cruder versions of it, *establishes* Marxism as monist-and-hence-also-
dualist rather than just complex and thus not monist and consequently not dualist either?[26] Or rather than pluralist-from-the-start
and, as such, in 'no risk of becoming dualist'? (I deliberately take
the chance of being misconstrued here: I do not intend, obviously,
a Laclau–Mouffian but an 'ordered' type of pluralism, a conception
of 'primacy', as set out both above and in the earlier essay.) This
question the authors do not even try to answer. Without an answer
to it, their account of Marxism is exactly as cogent as the argument
that all people are vegetarians, most of them, though, incomplete
vegetarians with a 'dualist' diet.

Methods of Construction

The sole – and intellectually unsatisfactory – basis of this dualist
rendition of Marxism is the one I went on to identify, and to
which Laclau and Mouffe's next point is addressed. I suggested
that it is only because they read the history of Marxism teleologi-
cally, because they treat certain concepts there as anticipating

themselves, that they can represent these, retrospectively endowed now with a particle of their own thought, to be incompatible with historical materialism – as their thought *is* incompatible with it. To this they have responded by saying that there is no other proper way than theirs to proceed. History 'is always history of the present', it is constructed by 'questioning the past from the perspective of the present'; 'there is not an *in-itself* of history, but rather a multiple refraction of it, depending on the traditions from which it is interrogated.'[27] This is, again, a sidestepping of the issue by assertion of an uncontentious but irrelevant truth. Or else it is something worse. Yes, the historian or social philosopher is not a blank sheet and so forth. Thus, if there are some today interested in notions of justice, they are entitled to reread Marx's work in the light of that interest and even to try to show that he was moved by such considerations himself though his texts overtly deny it. But they do, then, have to *show* this: by reference, precisely, to the texts, and their contexts, any independent evidence there might be about Marx's intentions, and so on. One cannot make any kind of history one wants out of the present and its perspectives. In practice (as always with this philosophical tendency) Laclau and Mouffe argue in exactly the manner of everybody else: as if their account of Marxism could be assessed by reference to *what it is an account of.* In that case, to establish a dualism here they need to demonstrate the logical *inconsistency* between, for example, Gramscian hegemony and structural-Marxist concepts of class; or between Leninist political alliance, or Trotskyist permanent revolution, or Luxemburg's mass strike arguments, or Althusserian overdetermination, and the same. But they do not and, I contend, they cannot, because there is none. They merely generate an appearance of inconsistency by denaturing these concepts and arguments into shades of another, future 'discursivity'. To react to this criticism by saying in effect, 'But that is our perspective, what else can we do?', is empty. One could do what others have to do, meet criticism with argument and evidence, give reasons, if there are any, why the account of Marxism produced from within this perspective deserves to be taken seriously, *as* an account of Marxism – reasons beyond the bare fact of the perspective *being* a perspective.

Or... is the perspective indeed just sufficient unto itself? Are we dealing, in other words, with what the authors elsewhere in their text allege to be 'an invention of the fundamentalists', that is, with a relativism?[28] Quite probably. But it is impossible (as always with this philosophical tendency) to pin down, because by its nature it is – endlessly – equivocal about its nature, right down to the very deepest layers of thought. Hence, no 'in-itself of history, but ... a multiple refraction of it'. Of what, though? Let them have this as they please. If their account of Marxism *is* sufficient unto itself, there is nothing for the three of us to discuss here. They are welcome to that particular kind of dark security. But for my part, I will still do my best to persuade those who accept such terms that there is a gulf between Marxism as it was and is and the Marxism Laclau and Mouffe have 'constructed'.

We now have another insight into the methods of this construction. Their book maintains that it is a 'logic of the symbol' ('the overflowing of the signifier by the signified') that governs Luxemburg's conception of the mass strike and its notion of an interaction between the political and the economic. I dispute this. It is an ungrounded intrusion of their preoccupations upon hers. They claim I have provided no *argument*, merely an 'enumeration'. They refer thus to my detailed break-down of her ideas, in thirteen separate points. As it is my contention that they do violence to these ideas, how else should I argue the case than by setting out her view of the mass strike in as much detail as space will allow, so that readers then have the material – textual *evidence* – to judge for themselves as to the cogency and balance of the disputed interpretation? But Laclau and Mouffe have a different approach to these things. They 'would not disagree', you see, with my mere 'enumeration': it does not contradict anything in their analysis. But, strange to relate, from the experience of revolution, they then pick out for explicit mention that *and only that* which neatly fits their 'symbolic' interpretation: to wit, that a strike over wages can in certain circumstances symbolize opposition to the system as a whole; just as 'rose' can symbolize 'love'! Everything *else* in the enumeration, some dozen points, all other 'logics' or causalities – the strengthening of organizations by involvement of new layers of the working class, troops shooting striking workers, the effects of socialist agitation, the use of newly won political rights in further-ing trade-union work – they prefer not to talk about, much less explain for their readers. Thus can one aspect of a complex concep-tion be transmuted into its central 'mechanism'. And thus can you reply to criticism by saying exactly the same thing again with-out addition.[29]

That much on Luxemburg. But on the other Marxists whose treatment I criticized, there is even less. On Althusser: silence. On Lenin: silence. On Trotsky: ritual enunciation of the word 'theoretical' (italicized four times within a paragraph) to cope with the fact that the notion of relative autonomy is central to a text in which, it was alleged, he had simply fallen back on the greenness-of-life argument. One or two sentences isolated from their place in that text suffice to validate his reliance on the greenness of life. But half a dozen formulations of 'relative autonomy' in the same text (merely a brief reply to a critic) and the whole compara-tive historical discussion of the Russian and Western European states which supports them in his primary writings on this question: not, by Laclau and Mouffe's fine sense of proportion, a *theoretical* analysis. And on Bernstein, Sorel and Gramsci (joint subjects of two memorable paragraphs of untrammelled discursive play)? Silence.[30]

So, to the second criticism made of their book the best the authors have to offer are a couple more pure repetitions, unsullied by the strain of persuasive reasoning; and apart from that there are just some significant gaps in a 'point by point' reply; responses hardly better than the gaps since they succeed in either missing or dodging the point of *each* of the four points they pretend to respond to; a manifestly tendentious and self-serving characteriza-tion of the sort of account of Marxism *Hegemony and Socialist Strategy* contains; and then a little piece of demagogic attitudinizing.

3. Voids

My critique takes some care pointing out a deficiency at the heart of Laclau and Mouffe's social theory: in the notion of 'hegemonic articulation'. Unable, in their own terms, to conceive the identities articulated by a political discourse as either 'elements' or 'moments' (i.e., as constituted, respectively, outside or inside the given discourse) without falling thereby into an 'essentialism', they settle for them being something in between. I showed, however, what this means in practice: a systematic conceptual prevarication. Against the idea of a class delineation of identities, the *internal* (the constitutive power of the articulating political discourse) is urged, and all such external 'fixity' dismissed in favour of 'radical unfixity' and the like; as if the internal was just everything. But then against the articulating discourse being rendered into a closed totality, and in favour of 'pluralism', the *external* (independently and separately constituted identities) is appealed to and so some external fixity allowed after all. I argued: first, that there are no clear or consistent criteria of usage here, only usages of convenience, whether of fixity/unfixity, interiority/exteriority etc.; second, that the critique of Marxist assumptions in this matter is entirely vitiated because it *depends* on one side of the prevarication (that there is no external fixity) holding firm – Marxism has lived from the beginning with identities constituted *in part* politically; and third, that the conception is nearly vacuous, since it enables one to explain nothing about the relative fates of different political discourses except by falling back on other, including 'economistic' Marxist, categories. All of this is laid out over several pages – composing one sixth of the essay to which they belong.[31] I report Laclau and Mouffe's views in detail, the very core of what they positively put on offer. I develop these criticisms of them: methodically, step by step, in terms, I believe, of some clarity, and with substantiating quotation and full referencing. I engage at length with their ideas. The two of them respond more economically. They say nothing.

4. Norms

Then there is the matter, also, of the normative vacuity of their work. What are the grounds, I asked, for their usage of 'progress-ive'? What is the normative basis for *any* determinate political direction? – when the categories of progress, objective interests, 'the anthropological assumption of a "human nature"', 'universal discourses', have all been rejected. Laclau and Mouffe begin with a profession of pluralist virtue: if it is 'apodictic certainty' – as does not admit of any 'discussion' – that is being asked for, then there can be no such normative foundation. But there is still the 'possibility of reasoning politically and of preferring, for a variety of reasons, certain political positions to others.' Never mind about a certainty beyond discussion. As an 'epigone of Marxist ortho-doxy',[32] I would have, of course, to want that sort of thing. But, actually, reasons would be fine, ordinary discussable reasons, a 'variety' of them. What are they?

We get here, first, a brief discourse on humanism. The authors do not deny the validity of humanism's values, they say, but merely insist that these have been constructed over a long history. They prefer it, then. The paragraph devoted to it, however, is exclusively given to talking about the 'emergence' of humanism, this 'process of multiple construction', the 'various discursive surfaces where it has taken place', and so forth. But *that it was constructed* cannot itself be a reason for preferring it. As I do not have to tell Laclau and Mouffe, everything of this sort is constructed; hence also the 'racism, sexism, class discrimination' by which, they observe, humanism is threatened.[33] Perhaps they think that referring thus – from the outside – to the production of humanist values in positive terms sufficiently acquits them of any obligation to expli-cate reasons. But there is a small difficulty with this. For, *the* value they single out so to refer to is the humanist concept of 'Man', no more, no less: the '"human being", without qualification'. They do not trouble to explain how one such concept of 'man' can be adjudged better than another once a *human nature* has been excluded, just what in that case *are* the reasons for preferring it;

how, indeed, you can *think* a concept of 'man' – from the inside – without 'any anthropological foundation'. The contradiction is dazzling and merely generalizes that which I had already drawn attention to: their appeal to a notion of *human* capacities, but without any human nature. If ever there was a threadbare orthodoxy of the left, whether Marxist, structuralist or 'post'-either of them, supported intellectually today by nothing but the force of constant reiteration, it is this denial of a human nature. Having spent the best part of three years on a painstaking argument, reason by itemized reason, against it, I do not think too highly of little homilies about certitude and reasoning from people whose own level of argument on human nature is the 'presumably a gift from heaven' one. For the rest, that the authors' outlook might draw determinate normative content from an indirect reliance on assumptions they overtly reject, I already pointed out. The resulting self-contradiction and the 'indirection' are now given a new – and extraordinary – expression: external endorsement of humanist discourse about 'man' in a discourse about discourses, because 'man' in a presentation of reasons is inadmissible, having been expelled under another name.

And we get here, second, a recapitulation of Laclau and Mouffe's notion of the democratic revolution. It is another discourse about discourse. For, if you search this recapitulation for what it is they might construe as supplying reasons for the (democratic) political position they prefer, all you will find is the following: that the relation of worker to capitalist is not intrinsically antagonistic but only rendered so in terms of democratic discourses of equality and rights. This is an enhanced argumentative mode: pure unenlarged repetition, as several times before, but now without even signalling that there has been a criticism – as though the repeated just needed no defence; rather than masquerading as the defence of itself. The capitalist-worker relation may well be transformed into an antagonism (and, thereby, an oppression etc.) in the terms of one discourse. But in the terms of another it is not; and in the terms of yet others there is virtually no relation, as I showed, that cannot be construed as antagonistic in this way.

So the notion of antagonism as such yields no specific normative orientation. We still need reasons for preferring this discourse to others. Now, try to present equality *as a reason* – and not mere object in a 'sociology of discourse' – in a way that depends not at all on any, even minimal conception of human nature, or of basic human needs or human qualities; nor at all on principles of fairness or justice of quite general, that is, universal, scope. The discourse of equality and *human* rights is a 'universal discourse' if such there be at all; of the sort Laclau and Mouffe aver has had its day. They are utterly bereft here, by their own facile dismissals deprived of anything which could be given as a reason.[34]

What we have before us is not so much an answer to criticism as an abject debacle: a discourse *about* reasons, incapable of articulating any; a theory *of* discourses effectively speechless, unable to conduct one.

5. Essences

The cause of it, this moral vacuum, this strange, evasive, second-order talk, is plain: anything Laclau and Mouffe might venture as a reason directly out of their own mouths would be an 'essentialism'. The cause is their prodigal use of this last notion. Objective interests: an 'essence'. Human nature: an 'essence' (and so, it follows, *essential* human needs). Progress: an 'essence'. Marxist class: an 'essence' – and relations of production: an 'essence'. The party: an 'essence'. Revolution: an 'essence'. Society: an 'essence'. Separately constituted 'elements' of the social: 'essences' ... Without an effort, and some criteria, of discrimination between organizing theoretical concepts and genuine reductionisms, this becomes a blight on serious thought, an obscurantism. One can maintain that there is a human nature, to return for a moment to that, without making it the source and centre of all things, without denying the complexity of the social, etc. It has a certain, not altogether unimportant, explanatory role, that is all. And even categories with a very important explanatory role have to be shown to be more than just this to establish an 'essentialism'. They are indispensable to purposeful enquiry. But Laclau and Mouffe find reductionist 'essences' everywhere, even where there are explanatory categories they *know* to be less than exhaustive for the thinker who uses them. There is not a social theorist, Marxist or otherwise, of whom it could not be 'shown', up to standards equivalent to theirs, that his or her thought was 'essentialist' – though not fully so, and hence dualist as well. I have already proposed the gist of such a demonstration for their own thought. This entire line of criticism and questions, however, a clear presence throughout my essay – why discourse, all-pervasive, is less of an 'essence' than class; why what Bernstein continued to allow to Marxist categories sufficed to land him with a dualism, when the authors can fall back on these at need and that is all right – they have chosen to meet with another quiet absence in their own.[35]

6. Politics

I drew attention to a tendency of the authors to write of Marxism as though democratic concerns and principles were just foreign to it: to conflate the tradition as a whole with its authoritarian forms, so discounting its other, democratic heritage. This is, of course, a quite widespread tendency with non- (and especially ex-)Marxists, but it is by no means universal amongst them and of interest, therefore, coming from writers who profess a residual linkage to their Marxist past. Anyhow, I took issue with a way of talking about Marxism that effectively equates it with Stalinism. Laclau and Mouffe's 'reply' to this is rather special. Has Geras not heard of Stalinism? they ask; and the one-party system, press censorship, other such things? It may be wondered how such a 'reply' is possible in the circumstances. Easy. They report one sentence from my argument: that I – in common with very many other Marxists – 'take it as axiomatic that socialism must be democratic'; treat this as meaning that I hold the relation between socialism and democracy to pose no problem; and they are off. What about Stalinism? What about tanks? It is not axiomatic for anyone 'who does not live on Mars'; or 'in Gerasland'... and so on. Nothing, not in my text, not in theirs, no sense of care or just plain decorum, restrains them from the exigency of the instant; the quick, cheap riposte – the most fatuous vulgarity. They just ignore: the whole context of these words of mine they bring to the reader's notice; the fact that it is by contrast, *explicitly*, with Stalinism – and with 'the forms and pretensions of "actually existing socialism"' – that I emphasize the democratic heritage of Marxism; the fact that but two pages earlier in their own text, it was belief in the Soviet bureaucracy's 'betrayal' of the revolution I was being berated for, so that I did know about Stalinism, *then*. Nothing of this matters. How you 'construct' things is how they are. On the basis of one sentence I am representable as thinking what I do not. That releases our authors from the need of any genuine reply, in particular from having to decide either to defend or to correct the one-sided picture of Marxism and democracy they have presented.[36]

Laclau and Mouffe will have trouble finding, in my critique of them or in anything else I have written, a real piece of evidence that I think the relation between socialism and democracy is unproblematic; which is why they are obliged to construct one. They will find, rather, an abiding concern with questions of socialist democracy, and an understanding of the necessity of socialist pluralism that goes back a long way before 1985: formulated unambiguously a decade earlier; learned partly, it is true, from sources outside Marxism, but also from discourses within it; basing myself on which I some good while ago engaged critically with, to reject, the problematic of *the* party (without a single reference, it should be said, to 'essentialism').[37] And this was precisely the point of my statement they so traduce: that a socialism that is democratic is not only thinkable, but has been much thought, within Marxism; has been a central aspiration, goal and project there; an integral, continuous strand. Any account of the tradition that suggests otherwise is worthless. That is not to say there are no problems for contemporary Marxism in this area: relating, especially, to the need for more precise theory about the institutional shape, the regulative norms, rights and procedures, of a socialist democracy; for a prospective map of the constitutional order of feasible social-ism. But Marxism has no special burden to bear here vis-à-vis other currents of socialist thought. This is a common question for them – us – all, a rather large one. Some sobriety before it, a certain fair-mindedness and balance in assessing the relative records of different socialist traditions, would not come amiss from authors who, as I observed, themselves offer virtually nothing to-wards such a map, repeating all the while, '*radical* democracy'. This, the main point in my comment on their views on democracy, they prefer, yet once again, to step around, in order to focus on a single prefatory remark interpreted in their own inimitably free way. Except... that they now offer for our edification a formula – 'the consolidation and democratic reform of the liberal state' – whose radicalism would scarcely embarrass the Rt. Hon. David Owen.[38]

What *is* it, though, that keeps reproducing this (at every turn, every point), the nimble side-step? According to Laclau and Mouffe, I represent them as seeing communism and fascism as identical 'types of society'. But that is not what I said. Which was: that they use 'totalitarianism' as denoting something *common* to a politics of the left and fascism, and whose source, with respect to the left, is located within the logic of Marxist theory itself, because within 'every attempt to establish a definitive suture'. Responding that communism and fascism are not identical types of society is child's play. It spares them, again, having either to defend or to amend the thesis that totalitarianism is inherent in the very nature of Marxist thought. This raises an interesting question. Their essay of 'reply', though it withdraws not one of the *specific* disparaging theses about Marxism with which *Hegemony and Socialist Strategy* is thick, has taken on, oddly, a certain greater friendliness of tone towards it, at least where vague, unfocused *generalities* are concerned. Laclau and Mouffe talk at the end, for example, about 'giv[ing] to Marxism its theoretical dignity'. They ought, then, to say whether this is or is not the dignity of having been responsible for show trials, mass purges, the Gulag and the rest.[39]

Diversions (I) – Existence

No reader of my essay could possibly mistake what its main concerns were: to contest the authors' rendition of Marxism and criticize the social theory they now prefer. This is fifty-three pages of fifty-six, 95 per cent of the body of the text. The other three pages were given to a certain matter of ontology: whether objects exist external to thought. After some introductory remarks, Laclau and Mouffe begin by devoting fully 40 per cent of their response to those three pages. Why? The issue addressed there is an important one, doubtless. But in view of their failure to reply to anything else; not even the pretence of a reply, just complete silence, on two of the principal criticisms (concerning elements/moments and subordination/antagonism/oppression) of the social philosophy they offer; one cannot help wondering about what really governs the sense of proportion here. In any case, on *this* question they are not short of what to say. We are taken through the philosophers, authorities ancient and modern: Wittgenstein, Hanna Fenichel Pitkin, Popper, Kuhn, Feyerabend, Richard Rorty, Aristotle, Plato, Berkeley, Hegel, Charles Taylor, W. T. Stace, Marx, Heidegger, Derrida, Saussure, W. V. Quine and Nietzsche. And where do we arrive? Just exactly where I said we were when we started: the authors formally affirm the existence of objects external to thought, but the rest of what they say cancels this out, robs it of any theoretical weight. For, once you try to give some content to these objects, you are dealing with their 'being' rather than their 'existence' and being is discourse-specific, discourse-relative. You cannot say anything *about* what exists outside thought, only that things do. I engage merely with the argument.[40]

But racking up a couple of silences of my own now in return, I will not be discussing: (a) Whether Laclau and Mouffe are philosophical 'idealists' in the *true* meaning. If they want not to be that, who am I to quibble over a word? (b) What could have motivated the patronizing dissertation – and its companions – that a football is only a football 'within a system of socially constructed rules'; as though I had imagined there to be some pre- or extra-social footballs, just primordially such.

Let us take, however, stones. If there were no human beings, the authors say, 'those objects that we call stones would be there nonetheless; but they would not be "stones"' – because of the absence of languages classifying and distinguishing them. Why the scare-quotes? The *word* 'stones', its meaning, cultural associations, human uses of actual stone, etc., would not be there. But if the objects we call stones would be there, then stones would be there, because they are the common referent of the expressions 'those objects we call stones' and 'stones'. Set that aside. If the objects we *call* stones would exist, would any of their properties with them? Such as make them a different kind of entity from, say, the one we call water, and such as would prevent what we call a bird from what we call drinking the first but not the second? If there is an affirmative here – that stones (for short) and water and birds would be differentiated by their properties even in the absence of discourse and so of classification – then part of what some philosophers call the being of objects seems to be right in there from the beginning with their existence. And if not, you cannot speak intelligibly about what exists outside thought *at all*: about inherent properties, what *was* the case in the prehistory of humankind. Existence has been emptied of all content to the benefit of being-discourse. It is easy to see why relativism could seem like 'a false problem' from within this perspective. Existence, so emptied, can be no external control for different versions of being, and the hope of any such control is misguided.

Now, reconsider this proposition: 'Subjects cannot ... be the origin of social relations – not even in the limited sense of being endowed with powers that render an experience possible – as all "experience" depends on precise discursive conditions of possibility.' I impugned the logic of it: it simply discounts one condition of experience (powers) on the grounds of there being another (discourse).[41] To the criticism that they here effectively annul the 'conditions of possibility' of discourse itself, Laclau and Mouffe respond by arguing that it is 'meaningless', 'absurd', to speak about 'the conditions of possibility of the being of discourse'. But I spoke of the conditions of possibility not of the being of discourse but of discourse, period. Do any such conditions *exist*? Such as natural powers, the biological make-up of humanity, a certain kind of brain? Laclau and Mouffe cannot say. They cannot say 'yes' without, again, putting a bit of what they call being back into what they call existence. But if such conditions do not exist, we will have to say all of nature is a discursive construction. *This* is what the two of them in fact do say. They say: 'natural facts are also discursive facts' – for the 'simple' reason that 'the idea [!] of nature' is historically constructed. And I say: this (like every) relativism is based on obfuscating the distinction Althusserians used to make between the real object and – the idea of it – the object of knowledge.

One other matter here. Forbearing to treat the two 'constructions' as on level terms, I take an earthquake to be a natural phenomenon and not an expression of the wrath of God; calling the latter construction a superstition. The authors opine on this account that I regard myself as 'a functionary of truth', an embodiment of 'the Absolute Spirit'.[42] I shall consider in turn the possibilities that this is not a serious argument and that it is. The grounds for taking it as unserious are that Laclau and Mouffe themselves plainly do not regard religious faith as an adequate basis for forming any kind of view about the world; which is why they can belittle the notion of objective interests or a human nature with 'chiliasm', 'heaven', 'God'; and me as a 'worshipper'. But when I say what they on some level also believe – and which has nothing to do, for me, with claims to absolute knowledge, transparency and so forth, and everything to do with what in the present state of our knowledge we have the best evidence for thinking – then we get this 'functionary of truth' stuff. It is the stuff not of argument at all, stuff only for touching up an image of Geras which this whole 'reply' is rather keen to establish, for want of a single argument of substance. One can only reflect, once more, on whether there are limits of *any* kind on the discursive 'patterns' these writers will permit themselves. Geras, it seems, must *not* voice the sort of assumptions about religious belief with which Laclau and Mouffe *do* scoff at others, including Geras – and do even here, in these lines where they so admonish him. For, as what does Geras see himself? Why, as an embodiment of the Absolute Spirit!

I now take the argument seriously, on the grounds that if the authors themselves take their discursive philosophy seriously, it is hard to see what reason they could have for differentiating in terms of truth value between the two 'constructions' of the earthquake and dismissing one of them as a superstition. Just two alternative discursive constructions of 'being', then. Here I pose a different question. How far are they willing to go in this direction? For, you see, you can say not only that an earthquake is an expression of the wrath of God, but also that AIDS is; or that famines, widespread poverty, are. We might regard the first, in that case, as due punishment rather than the consequence of a non-moralizing virus, and give prayer as the best way of dealing with the second. Laclau and Mouffe will not go this far. Why not?

Diversions (II) – Language

I did not mince my words in saying what I thought of the quality of the ideas and arguments in *Hegemony and Socialist Strategy*. Its authors disapprove, complaining that my essay belongs to a genre of denunciation. They invite their readers to decide what to think of me for 'such language'.[43] I bring this rejoinder to a conclusion with a few observations on the matter.

First, as to my denouncing them, I say the opposite is true.

I engaged *with their ideas*, arguing with these in considerable detail and over a space of more than twenty thousand words. They may not like the result of that engagement but no author has a right to expect only favourable results. They, on the other hand, as the foregoing demonstrates, have not done me the same courtesy: of responding squarely to the actual arguments I put forward. The complaint about denunciation is merely part of their effort to deflect attention away from the balance of *argument*, with an image which is itself purely denunciatory: epigone, denouncer, functionary, worshipper. This image, some well-chosen silences, a lot of intellectual wriggling and evasion, are made to stand in where the (harder) activity of responsible advocacy should be. Laclau and Mouffe make a bad mistake here, just trading on the stupidity of the reader – as though there were nothing outside their present discourse against which it could be gauged.

Second, as to the language itself which they complain of, I am disinclined, on further reflection and in the light of their 'reply', either to withdraw or to temper a single one of the epithets I used of their book. Indeed, nothing testifies more clearly to the aptness of those, nothing more clearly to the nature and intellectual standards of that book, than the poverty of what has now been produced in its defence. What words *are* apt to describe an intellectual approach which, criticized for posing the spurious alternative, *a* or *c*, when there is another possibility, *b*, responds by simply changing the alternative and explaining, 'you see, we do not say either-*p*-or-*r*, because in fact we think *q*'?[44] Which insists on a meaning for 'determination' that leaves no choice but between the most rigid economic determinism and unqualified plurality and – in the next breath! – charges a critic with dishonesty for saying that this is the kind of choice the approach imposes?[45] Which defends itself against the criticism of having distorted Marxism through the lens of its own preoccupations by appeal to the fact that its way of looking at Marxism is a way of looking at it? Which endorses (a discourse containing) the humanist concept of 'man', having rejected the anthropological assumption of a human nature? Which asks, has he heard of Stalinism?, of someone who says that there is another Marxist tradition *than* Stalinism? Which fends off the question of the conditions of possibility of discourse by calling it a meaningless question? 'Obscurantism', 'absence ... of all sense of reasonable constraint': that seems fair. And so does 'theoretically profligate, dissolute'; because such, I submit, is what we are faced with here, a kind of licentiousness in the realm of ideas. It has to be one of the more grotesque ironies of the recent history of socialist thought that the authors of all this are unembarrassed to pin upon themselves the badge of 'obstinate rigour'.[46]

I, for my part, therefore, now invite the reader to consider this question. How is it possible for two people, responding to criticism of *their own* work – for, who has a stronger interest than they in seeing the import of such criticism? – to contrive to miss the point not just of one or another, but of virtually every, argument put to them, piling evasion upon evasion, pure repetition upon pure silence, self-contradiction upon irrelevance, with never so much as one decent answer in what is supposed to be a reply? For reasons earlier stated, I do not impugn the intellectual honesty of these two people. I think there is a simpler explanation. They are just short of genuine answers. Unable to meet the criticisms made of their book, they recklessly thrash about for anything, more or less whatever, that might preserve a certain appearance, a certain external *form*.

Third: it is possible, of course, to express oneself more gently, tactfully, than I did and now do again. In most circumstances there is a lot to be said for that: for friendlier, less adversarial norms of debate. But I have to say that I did, and do, not judge the circumstances of this particular debate to call for any such emollience, my own perception of what was *casus belli* being rather different from the one implied by Laclau and Mouffe's expression of grievance in this matter. They would like to have it that there they were, two conscientious scholars quietly ploughing their own furrow, only to be viciously set upon by a rude sectarian and fundamentalist. By such injured naiveté I confess myself unimpressed. Over pages and pages – and some current back-pedalling by them about this notwithstanding – the authors of *Hegemony and Socialist Strategy* systematically rubbish the Marxist tradition, with their battery of '-isms', from 'essentialism' through 'monism' and 'dualism' to 'stagism' and 'classism' and 'apriorism' and a good few more, and with 'suture' and 'closure' and 'chiliasm' and 'fixity' and 'transparency', repeated again and again, relentlessly, conjoined, recombined, permutated.[47] It is hard to think of another book so rich, and at the same time so ugly, with a terminology of error; with such an ease in the use of it, on the flimsiest pretexts (wild antitheses and exegeses, for which no serious word can now be found as a defence) and in a way that just mocks the trouble, the worry, the difficulty, of mature intellectual work. Such is good enough for the wholesale depreciation of Marxist thought. But themselves subjected to a forthright language of riposte, Laclau and Mouffe cry foul, not very nice.

Fourth, their complaint, and the image of myself it is designed to feed, are part of a more general theme, a double and mischievous obfuscation, which should be brought out into the light. Marxism and Marxists, for aspiring to cognitive objectivity, are held to lay claim to certainty, absolute knowledge, transparent access to truth and so on; whereas the theory of discourses, being (what I call) a cognitive relativism, is supposedly undogmatic, open and plural- ist, *democratic*. This view of things simply conflates the aspiration to knowledge – shared by Marxism with the mainstream traditions deriving from the Enlightenment – with notions of intellectual finality and infallibility. But unlike faith or dogma, genuine know- ledge is always provisional, subject to revision in the light of new information and evidence, needing periodically to be restructured, fallible; open therefore to 'pluralist' discussion and criticism, yet at the same time, pending possible rebuttal or revision, *knowledge* so far as we have managed to get. The aspiration, and all claims, to knowledge, in the sense of it just explained, are democratic by their nature, because they have to satisfy rules of consistency, external reference, evidence, that are accessible in principle to all, *public and accessible* – if sometimes only with difficulty – *as are the realities themselves to be known.*

There is nothing democratic whatever, on the other hand, about a perspective that plunges these matters into utter arbitrariness and irrationalism. Laclau and Mouffe 'democratically' cut *everybody* off from access to what could meaningfully be called either truth or objectivity – with the single exception, dear to all relativists, of themselves. Overtly denying that there is any being-as-such, any in-itself, in terms of which competing discourses might be adjudicated, they install somewhere out of sight a secret tribunal of truth, mysterious in its ways, which allows *them* to judge here: as 'essentialist', hence *wrong about the nature of the world*; as economist, thus unable to understand the *reality* of the social; as determinist, therefore misconstruing history's *actual* openness, etc.; which allows them to employ a language of external reference, of objectivity, of truth (saying not 'that is how we like to look at it', but 'this is how it *is*, here is what *happened, these* are the developments') to tell us what is really what; which allows them that long, that tireless, that never-ending 'this is how it is' with which the relativist tells you why you cannot say 'this is how it is', so sending rational knowledge and consistency to the devil.[48]

There is another aspect to Laclau and Mouffe's complaint against me. It is that, 'absolutely definite about the psychological motivations that led [them] to write [their] book', I directly accused them of bending before careerist and political pressures, the pressures of self-interest and age. I did not. What they refer to here are the framing remarks of the introduction to my article, in which I raised *in quite general terms* the question of how far such pressures have been at work in the rightward drift of so many left intellectuals of my generation, and in the flight, within this, of so many of them from Marxism.[49] I freely concede that by placing these reflections at the start of an essay concerned exclusively with the critique of one book I may have created the basis for being misunderstood as I have. I did take some care, however, to emphasize that I was *not* putting in question the authors' integrity, as they themselves acknowledge but choose to discount. And such reflections are, in any case, perfectly legitimate ones; for anyone except she or he who imagines they are not subject at all to social pressures, that the pursuit of ideas is just exclusively that. Intellectuals can have a way of being extremely kind to themselves, ready to explain the behaviour of the whole world, but not to have their own situation within it exposed to discussion, as though they alone were beyond the pull of motives, disinterested, pure seekers. As a general issue, the question of pressures can reasonably be posed – especially in the social and political climate of today, and in face of numbers of quite unbalanced farewells to Marxism and indeed socialism, many of them lacking in intellectual substance. If Laclau and Mouffe just *know* this question is not relevant to their case, well and good. It is a confidence that sits oddly beside their dismissal of 'transparency' as a dream, and not one I would be willing to claim for myself. Still, I do not gainsay them on this. People can be moved just by the force or the flow, or by the play, of their ideas.[50]

But enough is enough. The two of them express a mock surprise that I should have devoted so much space to a book I judge so negatively. There is no cause for puzzlement. As a certain giant thinker contributed to explaining, the reach and the hold of ideas is not always a direct function of their truth or quality. Because he was not the reductionist he is so often represented as having been, he knew also that criticism of mystifying ideas is necessary, nevertheless, to trying to weaken the hold they have. In this case it is necessary for a quite particular reason. Laclau and Mouffe's insubstantial attack on Marxism and insubstantial alternative to it exploit the proper concern there is today about socialist agency. It has been put to me a few times, and it is something they themselves play on in both the introduction and the conclusion of their 'reply', that their thought is at least addressed to an important set of problems. Yes. But intellectual work has not yet become so easy that just addressing serious problems suffices to vindicate whatever they are addressed *with*.

Socialist thought is faced, today, with two broad kinds of difficulty. On the one hand, and as is only to be expected in consequence of the breadth and immensity of socialism's objectives, it is faced with problems of theory, of understanding; analytical and empirical questions, whether about the changing nature of capitalism, the forms and principles of a socialism worthy of the name, the movements, the moralities and the strategies that might have a chance of constituting it. It is now widely recognized, and amongst socialists of the most different persuasions, that answers are not so easy to come by. They are a long haul. The practice of producing or discovering them, as is also widely recognized, must inevitably be a many-headed, collective effort, in which open debate, a careful weighing of other viewpoints, innovation, revision and emendation, take their place beside commitment and enthusiasm. But socialist thought presently also confronts, on the other hand, a singularly hostile political and intellectual environment. It is pressed in from all directions by those ready to write it off, deride it, belittle both its hopes and its achievements as illusion or dross.

So besieged, socialist thought – in all its currents and varieties – has an even heavier responsibility than it should generally own to anyway, to conduct its discussions in a spirit of sobriety and just proportion and with a sense of the complex paths that truth and error alike persist in tracing across all straightforward maps of the historical intellect. Argument by caricature and simplification; by easy reduction and intellectual short-cut; by light-minded use of such hackneyed vulgarizations as have already been answered many times over (and as will be seen today for vulgarizations not only by Marxists but by a substantial number of fair-minded, non-Marxist students of Marxism) – this is a dual dereliction. It obstructs fruitful socialist debate. And it reinforces the currently difficult external environment of that debate. It is no fit style for the kind of socialist pluralism we need. In any case, enough is now more than enough.

Notes

1. Ernesto Laclau and Chantal Mouffe, 'Post-Marxism without Apologies' (hereafter WA), *New Left Review* 166, November/December 1987, p. 92.

2. Norman Geras, 'Post-Marxism?' (hereafter PM), at pp. 75, 77, 106 above. All page references to this essay are to the present volume.

3. WA, p. 92. For this and the next paragraph, see Ernesto Laclau and Chantal Mouffe, *Hegemony and Socialist Strategy* (hereafter HSS), Verso, London 1985, p. 84; PM, pp. 76–7; and WA, pp. 96–7.

4. PM, p. 111 – in reference to HSS, p. 117.

5. PM, pp. 73–5 (vis-à-vis HSS, pp. 139–40) and 100–102.

6. Emphasis here added. PM, pp. 75, 93.

7. For what follows, see WA, pp. 92–5.

8. PM, p. 74 – emphasis here added.

9. Ibid.

10. Cf. Raymond Williams, *Keywords*, Glasgow 1976, pp. 87–91. It includes, as if by foresight, the following: 'Matters of this degree of seriousness and complexity will not be settled by verbal definition but arguments about them can be thoroughly confused by insistent and pseudo-authoritative application of one fixed sense of this highly variable word and its derivatives.'

11. See David McLellan, ed., *Karl Marx: Selected Writings*, Oxford 1977, p. 389 (emphasis added); and Michael Evans, *Karl Marx*, London 1975, pp. 61–5.

12. See Leon Trotsky, 'What Next?', in *The Struggle Against Fascism in Germany*, New York 1971, pp. 144, 154–5, 158; Rosa Luxemburg, 'Social Democracy and Parliamentarianism', in Robert Looker, ed., *Rosa Luxemburg: Selected Political Writings*, London 1972, p. 110, and 'Social Reform or Revolution', in Mary-Alice Waters, ed., *Rosa Luxemburg Speaks*, New York 1970, p. 80; and cf. my *The Legacy of Rosa Luxemburg*, Verso, London 1976, pp. 51–63.

13. A brief comment on Nicos Mouzelis's contribution to this question. Though he too is concerned largely – but from his own angle – to defend Marxism against Laclau and Mouffe's criticisms, Mouzelis contends that there is 'a type of reductionism ... inherent in all Marxist discourse'. This is because even overtly non-reductionist Marxisms, such as stress the relative autonomy of the political sphere, still subject the latter to a subtle 'downgrading'. By contrast with the economic, which is treated as a site of structural determination and as capable of theorization as that, the political becomes the site of pure agency and conjuncture and so its differential forms or 'modes' are not theorized in their own right or given, in practice, the sort of weight conceded in principle in the affirmations of relative autonomy. As follows from what I say in the text, I do not accept this. What is true is that theories of the political within Marxist thought are still very underdeveloped. But the suggestion that the political sphere is simply reduced in all Marxism to a kind of untheorized, rolling conjuncture, with no real explanatory force being granted to different political *forms*, does not square with these arguments regarding the specificity of both fascism and parliamentary democracy. They concern precisely *types of state*; (in Trotsky's words) 'different systems of ... domination' and their differential effects. Mouzelis himself, it may be noted, treats Marxism's theoretical underdevelopment in this area as remediable, so permitting that the reductionism I think he wrongly alleges is not after all actually 'inherent' to historical materialism.

See Nicos Mouzelis, 'Marxism or Post-Marxism?', *New Left Review* 167, January/February 1988, pp. 108, 117–21.

14. HSS, p. 13; PM, pp. 75–6.

15. WA, pp. 95–6.

16. HSS, pp. 12–13; PM, pp. 91, 102–3.

17. HSS, pp. 26 (and 29), 51, 69, 99; and 13, 69.

18. For what follows, see WA, pp. 97–9.

19. PM, p. 72.

20. PM, pp. 61–2, 80, 95.

21. Peter Gay, *The Dilemma of Democratic Socialism*, New York 1962, pp. 68, 72, 143, 151; Carl Schorske, *German Social Democracy 1905–1917*, New York 1970, pp. 17, 19; George Lichtheim, *Marxism*, London 1964, p. 290. Cf. J. P. Nettl, *Rosa Luxemburg*, London 1966, vol. 1, p. 205 – and HSS, pp. 30–31, 38–9, 41.

22. For a discussion of just *one* such weakness, see Part One of this volume.

23. WA, p. 99; and PM, pp. 72, 77–84. I have left aside here a useless quibble by the authors that their main focus was not economism but 'essentialism' – as if their history of Marxism had been at all neglectful of the first or this criticism of mine had failed to mention the second.

24. PM, pp. 84–6.

25. WA, p. 99; PM, p. 87.

26. PM, pp. 93–4.

27. PM, p. 88; WA, pp. 99–100.

28. WA, p. 85.

29. PM, pp. 89–92; WA, pp. 100–101; in reference to HSS pp. 8–14.

30. PM, pp. 92–6 (and HSS, p. 71 for the two paragraphs); WA, p. 100.

31 See PM, pp. 100–110.

32. WA, p. 81.

33. Why do they not say 'racism, sexism, classism' here?

34. See, for this section: PM, pp. 110–14, 120; WA, pp. 101–5 (and HSS, pp. 3, 116–17, 152–3, 181, 188).

35. PM, pp. 71–3, 84–6, 95, 103–4, 109–10, 114–15 and *passim*.

36. PM, pp. 115–16, 119–20; WA, p. 101 and pp. 103–4 n. 28.

37. See *The Legacy of Rosa Luxemburg*, pp. 183–5, 188–90, 193 and *passim*; 'Classical Marxism and Proletarian Representation', *New Left Review* 125, January/February 1981; and *Literature of Revolution*, Verso, London 1986 (in which that essay is reprinted), pp. xiii ff. and the essays in Part II.

38. WA, p. 105.

39. PM, p. 119; WA, pp. 105–6.

40. For this section, see WA, pp. 82–92; PM, pp. 97–100.

41. PM, pp. 101–2, 123 n. 69 (and HSS, p. 115).

42. See WA, pp. 89–90 n. 17.

43. WA, p. 81.

44. This is the structure of the 'reply' dealt with in 1 (i) above.

45. See, in turn, 1 (ii) and 1 (iii) above.

46. WA, p. 79. Even in citing the language of which they complain, Laclau

and Mouffe cannot be bothered to be too accurate: they leave off the qualifier, 'theoretically', from the adjectives, 'profligate, dissolute', and disconnect these from the elaboration of them that is their direct sequel in my text – viz., 'more or less any ideational combination or disjunction being permitted here, without regard for normal considerations of logic, of evidence or of due proportion' – part of which they then give *separately*; so allowing the impression that I have, perhaps, charged them with some sort of moral depravity. See PM, pp. 64–5.

47. For references, see PM, p. 121 n. 8.

48. I am grateful to Andrew Collier and Bob Fine for discussions on this point (and cf. Bob Fine, *Democracy and the Rule of Law*, London 1984, pp. 199–200). I also take the opportunity of here thanking my friend, Paul Cammack, for more general discussion of the various issues. None of these individuals, of course, is hereby implicated in responsibility for what I have said.

49. WA, p. 81; PM, pp. 61–4.

50. With reference to the introduction to my essay, Mouzelis writes: 'what is really crucial in the context of a debate such as this is less to ascertain the reasons, conscious or unconscious, behind an author's break with Marxism and more to establish the cognitive validity or non-validity of what he or she has to say.' (*New Left Review* 167, January/February 1988, pp. 108–9.) It is just because I think this that I devoted forty pages to arguing about the validity or non-validity of what Laclau and Mouffe had to say.

Index